GOD IS NO DELUSION

HOPE FOR THE WANDERING FLOCK

GWEN FRANCIS

BALBOA.
PRESS

A DIVISION OF HAY HOUSE

Balboa Press books may be ordered through booksellers or by contacting:

Balboa Press
A Division of Hay House
1663 Liberty Drive
Bloomington, IN 47403
www.balboapress.com.au
1 (877) 407-4847

Scripture quotations are from The Holy Bible, English Standard Version, copyright @ 2001 by Crossway Bibles, a division of Good News Publishers.

Print information available on the last page.

ISBN: 978-1-5043-0074-2 (sc)
ISBN: 978-1-5043-0075-9 (e)

Balboa Press rev. date: 01/06/2016

CONTENTS

PREFACE

I have struggled with this book. I know I have to write it, but I have not been able to get it right. The first version – "In the beginning" was meant for people in the Christian Church who would understand the background without a great deal of explanation. I knew what I was doing. I was passing on a message. Whether they believed me or not was up to them. The second part of my task was more difficult. I have to explain my story and the God I know in a way that is relevant to the educated masses of today. When I thought I had accomplished this, I sent my manuscript to a professional assessor who tried to help me.

"The whole MS lacks cohesion. Is it about evil? Is it the story of your life? What is your target audience? I think you would be better to tell an interesting story that is focused on your essential message. Lengthy quotes easily lose reader interest. I do not think the MS is anything like ready for publication in its present form."

So do I start again? Of course. Any thing I have been given to do for God has to be the best I can do. The God I know is not boring or disorganized and neither should I be. I am now writing for people just like myself, who are not perfect, but who care about other people and the planet, and want to be at least on the right side of the ledger when their lives come to an end. I'm telling them my story and my story can't be told without including my experiences with the force of evil.

<u>October 2015</u>

So now I am revising again. A publisher has warned me of the dangers of libel and invasion of privacy – anything that could possibly damage the reputation of a person, place or thing. My original instructions back in the 1970s, from the force that I believed was communicating with me, were that no-one was to be criticised or condemned, but the truth must be told. It is not possible to tell the truth if all references to times or places have to be deleted. I have done as much as I can, and I am sorry if anything I have written is embarrassing to any person or institution. This is not a piece of fiction where authors often include a disclaimer in opening pages that says that except in the case of historical fact, any resemblance to actual persons, living or dead is purely coincidental. I have to write the truth as I saw it - so instead of a disclaimer, I am making a claim.

CLAIM

S ome of the people or institutions connected with my story still exist, but I have tried wherever I could, not to identify the people involved in my experiences, not to criticize or condemn any person, group or institution involved. I apologize if any of the facts embarrass any person or institution. It is easy in hindsight to say that people involved at the time could have behaved in a different way, but the situation was new to all of us. I have nothing but praise for those at the time who had the courage to step into new territory, sincerely believing that they were working for God. It was very hard for them to introduce new beliefs, based on their own experiences, into the conservative arena of a mainline Church, but without their courage I would not have been started on this journey. I have had to include facts that are necessary for a reader to understand, verify or dispute my story. I do not want to hide events such as my family history, or my time in a psychiatric hospital. I have tried to keep to the facts, to tell the truth about what happened. I know that there are people who will claim there is no truth, but if their argument is correct, that particular claim can not be true either. Buddha put the situation simply, when he said that when wise men disagreed it was like blind men examining an elephant – Each was certain he was right because each had hold of only part of the truth. One had hold of the trunk and believed he was holding a snake. One was holding an ear and believed it was a fan. Another, feeling a leg, believed it was a tree trunk and one with his hands on the elephant's belly believed it was a barrel. One standing at the back, had hold of the tail and was certain it was a broom.

Reasoned judgement depends on an accurate knowledge of facts – all the facts. It used to be said that the camera does not lie – but with modern technology a picture can be altered almost beyond recognition. The same event can be photographed through many different lenses and taken from many different angles, but a photograph of a person sitting on a chair cannot be a true representation of the same person who was standing beside a chair at the time the photograph was taken. If it is claimed to be a true reproduction, then it would be necessary to do some Socratic questioning; to ask the motive for the claim - to ask about the claimant's past history - to ask about any previous deceptions – to ask who would gain by a deception. I am claiming that my story is true. Others may have seen the same events from a different angle, and may have a different interpretation of them, but I have written only the truth as I saw it at the time.

1

INTRODUCTION

It is 2015. I am ninety one years old and I have now finished the first part of the task that was given to me nearly forty years ago. I must now finish the second part and then I will be able to rest with a clear conscience. I was told I would be a prophet and a priest, but I found that hard to believe. Why me? I was told my work would be to write, but few people yet seem to want to read what I have written. I was given a task to do and that was to pass on a message for all Christians. I was told to go to the priests, but if they would not listen, I was to go to the people. Well, I have told my story to priests as individuals, and I have told the message to leaders of a mainstream Christian Church in the response they asked for to a proposed Covenant. I have had no acknowledgement that they have heard what I had to say. Now I have gone to the Roman Catholic Church as well, There has been kindly communication there, even though there may disagreement with some of what I say. Finally I am offering my experience and beliefs to you – the well-educated young (and older) of today who cannot accept all the traditional teachings of the Christian Church, - or of other religions into which you may have been born, but who accept there can be spiritual experience, and are examining all types of religions and faiths, looking for something you can believe in and use for guidance.

It would be much easier for me to put all my experiences behind me and say, "I must have been imagining it all. It did not happen," but the files are there, the diaries are there, the scraps of paper with writing on are there in my files - and the resource books, the results of my work, are there on my web-site and free to all over the internet. When I said "I'll wait for you," I thought maybe my task would be finished in ten years – later it was twenty years and now it is forty years and I am getting tired. I am still being told to be patient, but realistically I cannot expect to have many more years with my brain and body still active. My sight is deteriorating and modern technology is a worry for me. How simple it was to write something down on a sheet of paper, put it in an envelope and post it. Now I find it difficult to do the things my grandchildren take in their stride. Word processing, e-mails and attachments. have all become a part of my life, and I must admit that in some ways they are an advantage, especially when it comes to altering or adding bits to a piece of writing. There is a disadvantage there as well, because it would be so easy for someone else to add, change or delete a word or a sentence, and if it was not in my writing, or if there was not a gap in the written text, how could anyone else be sure that it was authentic? At least my diaries are authentic – in my own writing, and if anything is crossed out or changed I have usually initialled it. There are two books since the 1970s and I have started on a third. Do I really need to go into these details and issue this warning? Yes, because through my experiences, I know that I, and all mankind, am fighting against an active force of evil that aims to help us destroy ourselves. It can deceive the eye and confuse the memory. It delights in hatred and it encourages conflict between people of all kinds. It even pretends to be God.

I know this because I was allowed to experience the force of evil for myself so that I could write about it for ordinary people to understand. And I was told to write about the God I know for the same reason. The editor of a local magazine, writing about Easter recently, said that she had been brought up within a mainline Christian church, gone to Sunday school and been confirmed, but had never heard God's call. I would like to tell her that whenever she has been motivated to do something good to help another person or the environment, she has heard God's call. When she has chosen to do that good thing instead of looking the other way she has answered. If I were to write to her though, telling her this, the force of evil would suggest to her that I am a crank and my letter would end up in the rubbish bin, where I believe so many of my efforts to communicate with the intelligentsia have already ended – even within the established church.

So many of my contemporaries have died or are in rest homes waiting to die. The husband of a friend of mine died a few years ago. He was eighty-eight years old, and at our age we know we are coming to the end of our journeys, so we start to wonder what will be beyond our time here on earth. I can't say that I have been particularly worried about it. I have always been more concerned with this life than the next, but those of us brought up within the Christian religion have been told varying stories about the afterlife, and many receive great comfort in believing in a resurrection, and meeting people who have gone before us. In the Anglican creed we

3

say we believe in the resurrection of the body and life in the world to come. Other religions have their own beliefs, and it is not my task to try to alter anyone's personal opinions. All I have been instructed to do is to offer information and provide an alternative for those who are still wondering and wandering – like my friend's husband. I can only write here what I believe and why.

My friend's husband was brought up in the Christian church. He had a scientific mind and found it difficult to accept that all the teachings of the church are true. He was an "upright" man and a kind one, and tried to live a good life. Most people would say he had succeeded, but there was enough of his early teaching still sticking in his mind, that when he was approaching the end of his life, he was starting to worry about the wrong things he had done in his lifetime. I can't imagine there would have been many, but we talked about the fact that probably we have all done some things in our lives that we would not like to have brought out into public view. A very religious neighbour had been talking to him about the need for forgiveness, and it was evidently worrying him. We agreed about there being an unseen force beyond ourselves and that it seemed to be a force for good, but when I said I believed there was a force for evil as well, and that force also tried to influence us, he could not agree. "Well *****," I said, "It's like this. Like the Good Samaritan, you see someone in trouble and your first thought is that you should go and help. That is God or the 'force for good' speaking to you. Then another thought pops into your mind. 'If I stop to help I might miss the footy game. Someone else is sure to stop,' and so then you choose whether you will listen to God or evil. Over the course of our lives, I reckon that if we have done more good than harm we will be on the right side of the ledger and I think you would be well on the right side."

"You make it so simple when you put it that way," he said.

"Well, I have had to make it simple, because I have always taught children," was my reply.

Like a good proportion of people of our day, he was happy to accept God as the "force for good," but he could not easily accept a force for evil, and that is how evil becomes so powerful – by convincing people it does not exist as an active force. I have not taught children about an active force for evil, but I have tried to show them how, when they make choices, they should consider whether the consequences of their choices will help or harm people.

I have never consciously – until now - set out to teach adults about religion, though when I have been asked questions by those who are still wondering, I have tried to explain the God that I know and that I have known all my life. After experiencing the power of the force for evil, and so ending up in a psychiatric hospital, I have been very cautious about talking to the ordinary person about that force. Many of my friends in the Christian church however would accept it – but not all. Even a local church leader, with whom I had to discuss my work recently, had doubts. Explaining about God and the opposing force however, is the second part of the task that was given to me, and that I feel I need to get on with now, but I am caught between a rock and a hard place. My friends in the Christian Church are not going to be happy with what I have to write about some of the teachings of the Christian Church. My instructions were that I was not to change the message just because it would be unwelcome to those who receive it. I was not to promote divisions or assist in divisions. I was to help the church and the ordinary people of today understand each other. No-one was to be criticized or condemned, but the truth must be told, and I must write about the God I know who is the force for good, and about the opposing force of evil, in a way that could be acceptable to the masses of today. I had been puzzling over how to write about such things and how to get started when the answer leapt out to me from an article I was reading. "Just tell it how it happened," so I will go back to the beginning and start there.

The beginning

Not that I knew a great deal about God when I was young, but "the beginning" has to include my childhood. I think God took the place of the father I never knew. God was always there for me to talk to and tell my problems to. Orthodox church teachings played very little part in my knowledge of God, because the orthodox church had turned its back on my divorced mother, and my mother seemed to have turned her back on a God who had allowed her first child to die in the influenza epidemic after the first world war, and had allowed her much loved husband to become an inmate of a mental asylum with no hope of recovery, leaving her with a baby and a two year old to provide for during the Depression of the 1930s.

My first acquaintance with God had been through saying our prayers every night - ending with, "and make Daddy all better," but over the years, God had not made Daddy all better. We did not go to church. I do not know whether my mother had come from a particularly religious family but I do not think so. It was my father who was a member of the Baptist Church, and if he had remained with us we would have been brought up within that church, and so we had not been baptised as infants as we would have been in the church to which my mother belonged. When I was about seven or eight years old however, I decided I wanted to go to Sunday School because my friends in the village three miles away went to Sunday School. By this time we were riding ponies to school, so I was allowed to ride to Sunday School. It was a Methodist Sunday School, but took all the children who wanted to go. We learned about a God of love and the teachings of Jesus, the Ten Commandments and the "Blessed are theys." "Judge not, lest ye be judged," and "Whatever you have done to the least of these, you have done to me." Simple songs like "Jesus loves me," "Dare to be a Daniel," and "Onward Christian soldiers" reinforced the basic teachings. And my step-father – my mother divorced and remarried when I was 11 – was a Catholic who had been disowned by his church for marrying a divorced woman, but had often read us fascinating stories from a children's Bible, and so I had a broad knowledge of the Bible stories, if not a detailed one of the dogma of the Christian Church.

Through my secondary school days I belonged to "Crusaders," a school lunchtime Bible Study group, where the simple teachings continued – mainly about the kind of life God wanted us to live – what was right and what was wrong. As seniors however, our voluntary teacher introduced us to the "Blessing of the Holy Spirit." This, she told us, was a one-off special experience of intense feeling, bestowed on a person whose heart was completely emptied of self, and therefore open to being filled by the Holy Spirit. It was not given just for the asking. God chose to give it to those whose hearts were right with him, and who would be used to work for Him. I was to remember this many years later at the height of the charismatic movement when all around me people were talking of the "Baptism of the Holy Spirit." They were asking for the gifts that the Holy Spirit would bestow, and especially the gift of speaking in tongues, which at that time seemed to have become especially important to people who genuinely wanted to work for God. I could understand how they felt though, because as a teenager, I had desperately wanted to please God and please our leader. I had tried hard to empty my heart of self and I told the leader I thought I had received the blessing, even though I didn't really understand it.

I had never particularly wanted to work for God though. I had never wanted to teach Sunday School, and as I grew older and my education widened I could not accept some of the teachings of the church and I could not teach what I did not believe myself.

In my young days I was more influenced in my concept of God by the experiences I had had outside orthodox church teaching, but the Anglican church contacted us when I was twelve. That was the year I started secondary school, and in that year a new young minister had come to our parish, full of enthusiasm. He had rounded up all those on the periphery of the Anglican church, baptised those who had not been baptised, welcomed my mother back into the fold - in spite of her divorce and having married a Catholic in a civil ceremony - and finally he had taught us what the Church believed we should know. He had taught us creeds and arranged our confirmation, but as a family, we never became regular church attendants. God, however remained my private friend and confidant. By now World War 2 had taken over our lives. In 1941 I went to study at Auckland University where my Crusader leader had suggested I should join the Evangelical Union, but I did not feel comfortable there. As many such groups do, they took turns at praying aloud - and all my conversations with God since my childhood had been private ones, so I did not stay with them. Because of the war, and before I had finished my B.A. degree, I left university after two years in order to do a teacher training course and help with the shortage of teachers. I chose Home Economics teaching. We attended our small country church at Easter and Christmas and a few other times during the year, but most of my talking with God was done outside the church. Like most of us during the war there were many prayers quietly said by people who were not church-goers.

After the war my husband and I were married in the Anglican Church in the nearby town. Like me, my husband had a basic faith in God. Like me he came from a mixed marriage where his father, from a Catholic family, had married outside the church, and like me he had attended a community Sunday school, that in his case, had been run by the Salvation Army. Our children were baptised, confirmed and married in the Anglican Church. They had gone to the same community Sunday school that I had attended. In the years after the war, most children of the village went to the community Sunday School, but a time came when the separate denominations decided that children should attend church with their parents, and that Sunday School should be combined with Church. Children therefore, whose parents did not want to attend church, no longer attended Sunday school.

I continued attending church over the years, but never on a very regular basis. I believed that the teaching of Jesus was a good foundation for living and that the Church needed to survive to keep the teaching alive. I wanted to keep our local village church going. It was nearly a hundred years old and was part of the fabric of our village. I still had a strong belief in God as my personal friend, but I found it even more difficult to accept all the teachings of the Church. When friends questioned me, I always justified my position by saying that Christianity had been the greatest force for good the world had ever known, so the teaching should be kept alive, and to do that the Church had to survive. Life went on in the same way until the 1970s and the Charismatic movement.

At the time the Charismatic movement came to our parish I was on the Vestry of our church. The Vestry is the committee that is responsible for the practical work that has to be done. To be honest, I was on the Vestry because most of the others from our small church had had a turn, and no-one else wanted to attend the meetings. Most of the vestry came from the large church in the nearby town. We were only a small group whose church had flourished when people travelled by horse and buggy. Our village had once had seven shops and a railway station with five railway houses, goods sheds and cattle yards – and due to unspoken competition, our church had had a higher steeple than that of the first Anglican church in the town - but the village itself was now suffering from the fact that the two mile distance between it and the town was only a matter of minutes in a car. The parish had a minister who had evidently become influenced by the teaching of the charismatic movement and wanted to involve his congregation in it. At the time it was very controversial in mainstream churches. Many people were wary of discussing it. In our area, it seemed to be almost like a secret society, with secret passwords. If you were one of them, you were a Christian. If you had not been born again you were not a Christian. One of my friends who had been involved in the movement in a different parish said it would split the church. A group supported the minister, and finally he decided to hold what was called a "Life in the Spirit" seminar, where all those attending would have the opportunity to receive the "Baptism of the Holy Spirit." After all the talk, many of the congregation of our small country church decided that they were quite happy as they were and would not go to the seminar. Because I was on the Vestry, I felt that I should go to find out for myself the truth of what was going on, and anyway part of my job would be to help with the tea. The events that happened next are described in the account that follows, and are the reason why I believe in a force beyond ourselves. My experiences then and in the next few years provided the certainty that had been lacking during my adult life, but also led to my experience of, and understanding of, the force of Evil.

2

PROOF AND CERTAINTY

To my knowledge, no-one on the Vestry had spoken publicly about their own experience, so no-one in the Parish, except the initiated, knew what happened at these seminars, but when I told the Vicar about my experience he insisted that I would have to give a report to the church. When I protested that I did not speak publicly about my private feelings, he insisted that I should give a report at least to the vestry who were quite divided on the issue. I need to state here that nowhere do I set out to criticize or condemn either ministers or members of the church at that time. Some of my first instructions were, "No-one is to be criticized or condemned but the truth must be told." The people involved were very sincere in their beliefs and had the courage of their convictions. They were quite sure they were working for God. The document that follows is a copy of the report I wrote. Looking back I can see that nearly forty years has brought some changes in the way I think and write, but whatever I wrote has been the truth as I saw it at the time.

"Written on *********

To anybody who is interested to read this statement.

I am writing this down now, while events are still clear in my mind, so that later on, I will not be able to say, or other people to say, "It was not true. You just imagined it happened." Also that I will not let time add or detract to my memory of things as they were that night.

As you probably know, in my time on the vestry of this Parish, I have disagreed with the Vicar on the subject of confirmation, and with Bishop ******* on the subject of abortion, because I felt strongly enough to speak up for what I personally believed. I do not necessarily say I was right, but I believe in the quote, "To thine own self be true," and if a person feels strongly, they should have the courage to say so and not just go along with the crowd. I did not always have the courage, but events in my life have gradually given me that courage, and now I finish that quotation which goes on to say, "and thou canst not then be false to any man."

This is to prove to you that what I am about to write is the truth, neither emotional nor imaginative.

I started going to the "Life in the Spirit Seminar" because I considered that someone on the Vestry, who was able to look at things in an unbiased manner, should go and see for themselves. I had heard of people being harmed or upset by these seminars, and because I care very much about people's feelings, having been hurt many times myself, I was determined that nobody was going to be hurt if I could help it in any way. I was also determined that I was not going to be pushed into doing anything I didn't want to do, by the actions of people around me. If they wanted to throw their arms around each other, dance up and down and shout praises to the Lord, they could, but I didn't need to follow their example if I didn't feel like it. With this intention firmly fixed in my mind, I attended the first four evenings and found that the speakers didn't move me all that much, I enjoyed the singing, I became very concerned about the people in my group who were sincerely looking for help - which I didn't think I needed, except for the hope that I would regain that feeling of closeness to God, and God as my friend, that I had had most of my younger days.

I felt that the best thing I had received from the seminar was that I had begun reading the New Testament again, and making time in a busy daily life for a set period of quiet reading and prayer which we were asked to do. My prayers were short, my reading longer and more meaningful than it had been for years. I felt that, if nothing else, the Bible reading was giving me back what I had been missing in the rush of my life. I felt that some of the others were a bit too uninhibited for my liking, and maybe they were putting it on because they liked to attract attention to themselves, however I gave them the benefit of the doubt, and said to myself and others, "Well- good luck to them if they feel like that, but we're not all made the same."

I had been told I wouldn't get past the fourth night, but was determined to complete the course. I rolled up at the fifth night in some trepidation as to what was going to happen, but determined I wasn't going to be psyched into anything by anybody. We had bought booklets at the beginning of the course which outlined the study for each week, with Bible passages to read etc., and for the fifth night, the questions we were going to be asked, the promises we were to make and the prayer we were to say. There was nothing in these that we do not say in confirmation or our communion service, except for the last piece about asking for the gift of speaking in tongues, which my Bible reading consistently told me that not all shall do, and I honestly believed that I did not have the right to ask for any specific gift, but that I should ask for whatever God wanted for me. I stated this to anyone who cared to discuss the matter with me.

Instead of going off privately into our groups, we were all in our groups in sections in the parish hall, which was crowded. Our leader had brought with her a young woman friend of hers and by this time our groups were beginning to feel like a family, at least ours was, and I felt a very deep concern for the others in our group, that they would get from this "Baptism in the Holy Spirit" what they needed, especially the man who had the religious teaching of young people as his responsibility. I wasn't really expecting anything for myself, or even hoping for anything, except to feel a bit closer to God.

Our leader said she had never seen so many ministers in one place before at a seminar. When the time came for what they called "ministering in our groups," our leader began with the man and he answered the questions as we do at confirmation, and then said the prayer, ending with, "and give me back the gift of tongues." Our leader and her friend then put their hands on the man's shoulders and immediately he began to speak in a perfectly recognisable language. Recognisable as a language, I mean, although I didn't understand it. I have studied Latin through High School, passéd Stage 1 French at University, one of my daughters has done Stage 1 Maori, another is specializing in Maori at Training College. It seemed fairly recognisable as a Polynesian tongue. After ministering to the

16

lady, who like me, was very reserved emotionally and didn't speak in tongues, they came to me, asked me the questions which I answered, and I said the prayer until I came to the bit which said, "and give me the gift of tongues." After some hesitation, because I have never been able to pray in public – I used to sit through Evangelical Union meetings at University in fear in case some one asked me to lead in prayer and finally stopped going because of this – I said "and come close to me as you used to be – and give me whatever you have in mind for me."

I think maybe my leader was sorry for me, but she put her hand on my shoulder and began to pray for me. Then the other young woman placed her hand on my other shoulder, just the tips of her fingers at first and I felt something like electricity come from her fingers, then she put her whole hand on my shoulder and I felt a great warmth flow from her hand through my shoulder. After praying for several minutes they said perhaps I had some resentment about somebody or something which was holding me back, but I said, "No," and anyway, I was more concerned about the others in my group than myself, which was true. The other young woman said, "Go for a walk on your own when you get home when you'll be able to relax," and we were all so delighted for the man in our group who was glowing with joy.

The evening continued with us later putting our hands on our teachers and praying for them, and later all the ministers putting their hands on (our minister)[1] and praying for him. There was nothing offensive, everyone was very sincere, and I was still determined not to be psyched. More songs and then ****** gave me the nod to make

---

[1]   I used our minister's first name)

17

the tea, which I did and thought it would be cold before they'd knock off to drink it. We went home. I commented to a friend I'd taken with me, that I had not asked to speak in tongues, and found that she hadn't either. We both concluded our leaders had been a little bit sorry for, or disappointed in us. I got home, found my husband still up, told him over a cup of coffee what had happened, and that there was definitely a power of some kind in that room and I had heard a man speak in something which was a recognisable language.

I might add that I had made the comment to ****** before the seminar even started that I had no real desire to be given gifts, because to me, too much responsibility would go with them, and I didn't really want the responsibility. I went to bed thinking I might have trouble getting to sleep, but was very tired and dropped off. A couple of hours later I woke up and found my heart pounding and thrilling with emotion. I felt as though my arms were reaching out to embrace the whole world, and there was enough love in me to surround and enfold all mankind. I thought, "Why me, Lord? Why me? I didn't ask for this. Why me?" Tears were running from my eyes and I thought, "Oh help, if I'd known this was going to happen I'd have taken a heart tablet before I went to bed. My bad heart is not going to stand for too much of this," and I wished it would stop for my heart's sake. It didn't though and my lips were moving, but I wasn't going to make the effort to speak. I felt I had much more than the gift of tongues, and suddenly and perfectly clearly, I knew the answer.

It was love. That is what it was all about. The <u>power</u> of love. If anyone has felt the power that draws two people together, and how strong that power can be, they can have a faint idea of what I mean. Imagine that power magnified to the size of God's love for mankind.

Infinite love and infinite power and it is real. (I think it only takes a slight step forward in faith and perhaps a willingness to love your fellow man. This is <u>my</u> thought. The rest is just as it happened)

Yesterday was too full of the problems of everyday living to have time to write, but my heart was still bothering me. I had to call around to the Vicarage with a message, saw ****** and told him I hoped he had got as much out of the night before as I had. When he questioned me, I told him what had happened, and that I knew without doubt and without question that the answer was the power of God's love – and that if this experience had happened at the meeting I would have decided I had been "psyched", but because it had happened at home I knew it was the truth and a logical answer which I would be able to believe with my intellect and not something emotional which would pass.

***** said I would have to testify to what I had told him. I said, "You know how I hate revealing my private emotions in public," and he said "To the Vestry anyway, it will have to be told," so this is my testimony, the true story of what happened, and while I have been writing this, I have been compelled to stop at least four times, and believe this also --- speak in tongues --- as a proof to me that what I write is true.

Luckily I don't know what language it is, because I said many times that if God made me speak in Chinese, I would believe he wanted me to go to China as a missionary, and I thought there were more unbelievers here."

------- the document ends.

My signature comes next and on each page there are my initials and the initials of my doctor to whom I went the next day to have his opinion as to whether I was of sound mind, and responsible for what I had written. These are the words on the report he wrote for me –

> This is to certify that after talking to Mrs Francis and reading her account, I can certify that her mind is perfectly clear, and that while she is very happy, she is certainly not imagining any of this. These events really happened to her.
>
> Signed –W. Smith.

This was written on the official notepaper of the doctors' rooms, and dated, and though that particular doctor is dead now, a record may still exist in the archives of the same medical centre.

Reading that report over again so many years later, I cringe a little at some of my expressions, but it was not meant to be an official document. I was middle-aged and had spent most of my life in a rural community. It was only a personal report written without editing, and written for a small group of people I knew reasonably well. I never expected it to go beyond that meeting.

Because I had to give this report publicly to the vestry though, I did not want to say anything in it that would embarrass anyone, or that would expose the feelings or actions of anyone else who was present, but now the whole truth needs to be told. In that hall that night I saw one person, one of those whom I would call the "pure in heart" standing transfixed with a look of pure rapture on her face. I also saw a group of mainly younger people, in a circle, whirling round and round, also appearing to be under the influence of some unknown power. The things I saw and heard that night, and those I later experienced for myself, convinced me once and for all that there is a power outside ourselves that communicates with us, that cares about us all, and that chooses certain people for certain work in this world.

One of our ministers recently has argued that the prophets were merely people of wisdom who worked out for themselves the things they told the people. From personal experience I know that just as they themselves had claimed, the prophets were chosen and could not refuse to pass on the messages they were given. Most of them had had no desire to be messengers, and most of them suffered for it. As far as I was concerned I do not think I was particularly wise at the time. I had made mistakes like most ordinary people do. Any wisdom that I gained later came from God showing parables to me, mainly through nature, and He was able to do this because of my way of life. At that time I spent a good part of my week-days working alone on the farm. Not too many people today do that, and if they do, they often have ear phones of some kind that fill their heads and minds with music. Because of the silence around me God was able to lead my thoughts in the direction He wanted, until I saw what He wanted me to see. I was not consciously meditating, but I suppose that is what happens when people do meditate. It frees their minds to receive inspiration from elsewhere. If academics and scientists are really seekers after truth they should research the similarities of experience of the prophets Anyone who believes that "God" is only a construction of the human mind should take a look at the lives and stories of the prophets, and they might find reasons to wonder about the possibility of a spiritual force that exists beyond and within our living selves - and leaves the body at death.

Though I have photocopies of the documents I wrote at the time, I believe the originals were in the folder that I gave to a leader of the group of ministers who were with our vicar on the day that they performed an exorcism on me. The Vicar had asked for this exorcism later on because I kept telling them they were handling the power that God was offering in the wrong way. Everyone else in the group seemed to be full of joy, and endeavouring to "speak in tongues" or feeling upset because they didn't, but after that first experience of infinite love, there was little joy for me. The leader of the group on the day of the exorcism was from out of our town. He said he loved me, and I said that if he loved me he would read what I had written and I gave him my folder. Whether he ever did read it, I do not know. Probably he is dead now, but possibly my papers still exist and they would be proof of what I believed God was telling me then to tell the church. At the time I did not know how important such a thing might turn out to be. I have only gone along one step at a time, but God always uses our mistakes for good in the end, so I have no doubt that He has everything under control.

Though it will interrupt my story, I need to include a piece of writing here so that no-one will be misled by anything I wrote then or at any time in later years. Later in 1980, I wrote a comment on the report, which shows how we must keep searching for the truth with open minds. The facts of what happened did not change but my own knowledge widened and my interpretation changed slightly.

* * * * * * * *

"Reading this report over again in 1980, I can see that the truth as I saw it then is not exactly the truth as a see it now. Facts do not alter, but knowledge and understanding may increase and so allow our interpretation of facts to be changed.

On page two of the report I said that I believed that everything the Bible says and teaches us is completely true. Now, after a great deal of study of the Bible and a far greater knowledge about the Bible and how and when it was written, I would have to say that the truth is there and if we go to the Bible genuinely looking for the truth God will show it to us. Of course, if we go to the Bible looking for a verse that will support our own opinions, we will also be able to find one. The people who wrote the books of the Bible were people just like us, and they wrote the truth as they saw it then in the light of their own understanding. Just as their knowledge of God increased from the picture that the people of the Old Testament had of Him to the picture that Jesus gave us of Him, so we need an updated picture for today. We need to use our increased scientific knowledge in our study of the Bible and go on searching for the truth. St Paul said, "We see through a glass darkly." We cannot take an isolated theme and say, "This is the truth." It must always be held up against the overall picture of God's concern and care for individuals and the world He created for them."

* * * * * * * *

That was how I had come to understand the Bible in 1980 through my own experiences.

Going back to University in 1995 to study world religions and their sacred writings only increased my belief in one force for good that has communicated with human beings right from their beginning wherever and whenever that was, guiding their evolution from some drop of material to the creatures they are today – with brains and free will - with the power to choose between good and evil. I speak of God as "Him" for want of a better way of describing the force I know. As well as being a force for good I do not see God as a specific person, (for example an old man sitting on a throne) though I know that part of His being is a mind that knows and cares for each of us as individuals. Perhaps that is what He is – a mind of some infinite kind. As I was shown once – "All things to all people for all time according to their needs."

There is a tree on my farm that I can see from my window now[2]. It is a macrocarpa, a hundred years old and has an enormous spread of branches. Cattle shelter under it from the heat in the summer. It is much wider now than it was in 1980 and I wonder how long the branches will be able to survive the westerly gales that come in from the coast. Back in those earlier days of my education about God, a mob of young cattle were sheltering under it one day and I was shown that that is how God is – an umbrella over mankind. I took a photo of it then to put in my diary – along with the oak tree with the two branches, one of which was going to survive and become the leader. I wonder if the trees themselves will survive until people read my story. I wonder if the message I was given to pass on will be heeded, and if the Christian Church will divide like the oak tree, and the branch that God chooses will flourish. In the beginning I would have said, that with God all things are possible so of course it will flourish, but now I know that God gives us the opportunity and will help us, but we have free will and will need to take the first step. The second message that was dictated to me showed me the frightening alternative.

---

[2] Photo on this page. The photo of the oak tree that divided is on page 23

1998 The tree that was large enough for all to shelter under.
God as an umbrella over all mankind.

3

THE LESSONS CONTINUE

The "Life in the Spirit" seminar was just the beginning of the story that has gone on over the many years since then. Sometimes I had vivid dreams that contained messages for me. Sometimes words spoken by other people or on the television gave me messages. I was told that I was to serve God by writing and teaching, but I had a long way to go and a lot to learn. Once I had accepted what was happening to me I started writing down everything I was shown on any scrap of paper that was at hand. Later I kept a diary and wrote down all the parables and messages that God had shown me. Usually they have been perfectly clear. I would see something happening in nature or in the society around me, and I would be shown perfectly clearly in parable form what it meant for the church or mankind. Perhaps that is the gift of knowledge, or perhaps it is as Jesus said – "Let those who have eyes see and those who have ears – hear." That is how it has been for me. It is like a flash of knowledge. It comes so quickly and clearly that I would never have had time to think it out for myself. The rest of the time I have my own opinions of course, and they are as human as anyone else's. I think it must have been like that for many of the people who wrote the books of the Bible. When I read Paul's writings, I can see flashes of writing straight from God, like his piece on love in Chapter 13 of his first letter to the people of Corinth, and in other places I can see a man of his times writing his own opinions - particularly about the place of women.

I often have to check what I have written. I was told right from the beginning that nobody was to be criticized or condemned, but the truth had to be told. No-one was to be blamed for doing what they thought was right, but to know what is right and not do it is where we go wrong. I have tried to keep to those instructions, but I must admit that, not being a saint, it is difficult to keep my mouth shut at times, especially when I see anyone being hurt, especially children, or if I see the power that I know as God, being misrepresented. At least when I write, I can have second thoughts about what I have written, and have more control over what people will read – and now, my computer will add or delete as required.

Before I go on to explain the God whom I came to see more clearly as my lessons continued, I need to explain also that, like my friend's husband, I had not particularly believed in an active evil force such as Satan, or whatever names have been given to such an entity. I had not seen life as a battle between good and evil. My experiences in the months after the blessing of the Holy Spirit changed that forever. It was necessary for me to experience it for myself so that I could explain it simply to others. To me, God is the force for good in the world, but there is also an opposing force for evil. God loves us with an infinite love, but the malevolence of the force that works against good is so horrifying that it is difficult to imagine. Even now, so many years later, the memory of the flash of malevolence that God allowed me to feel, makes me shiver. Not that I need to fear it as much as I did at first when it was new to me, but if we are going to be able to fight against it, we need to recognize and understand the enemy that is there. I can see it at work in the actions of those who perform the atrocities like beheadings that we see on our T.V. news and equally in the stubborn refusals of leaders to compromise -stubborness that result in so much misery for refugees caught up between warring factions in Africa and the Middle East today.

Evil's most powerful weapon is to convince us that it does not exist as an active force. Another of its weapons is to pretend that it is God speaking to us. We can see this if we think of the cruel and harmful things that have been done in the name of God, Allah, or Jehovah or any other more primitive god over thousands of years and that are still being done. The true God – the force for good that I know - would never ask one human being to harm another, but evil - pretending to be God, can convince people to harm each other in the name of their particular god – and leaders can convince their followers that harming others is what their god requires of them. It will even reward them for it. The God I know would never have required Christians to burn other humans at the stake or torture them into confessions of heresy. Protestants versus Catholics in Northern Ireland have been a more recent example of evil's promptings. Those young suicide bombers today who have been told by their Islamic leaders that they will be rewarded in Paradise for their actions will be disillusioned, but too late to prevent the harm that they will do. As for the leaders who incite cruelty and violence in the name of their gods, they do not often carry the explosives themselves - but it is not my place to criticize or condemn. God will be the judge, and maybe the punishment will be their wasted lives and the suffering of their own families and those around them..

An author quoted in an interview a few years ago[3] said, "It was obvious what our parents were for – to beat the Nazis and keep the idea of democratic civilization alive. I assumed as a child that we would have a similarly big grand task, but with the end of the Cold War I thought – but what are we for now? It seemed empty and strange."

Young people do need to have a "grand task." We do still have a common enemy and we need to know that that enemy is the force of evil.

Many people in the western world today may see Islam and its terrorists as the threat and the new "grand task." That is the front we see, but the problem is further back than differences of religions. Religions evolved in different places in answer to different needs, but it is the same force for good that has been behind the ethical teachings of those religions. Islam advocates justice and equity: it teaches that brother should not fight against brother, but it was not too long after the death of Muhammad before a power struggle over who was the rightful leader split Sunni and Shi'ite Muslims into factions that seem to take pleasure today in blowing each other up. I can see the force of evil encouraging them in the name of Allah. Religious leaders will need to accept that our fight in future is not against other cultures or religions. It is against the force of evil that deliberately sets out to instill hatred and fear of others, so that humanity will destroy itself. All the fruit of evil such as hatred, greed, selfishness, envy, laziness

---

[3]   Sebastian Faulks – in Canvas, N.Z. Herald 22.3.2008 p22

and especially apathy can be used by evil to influence people in many ways, and this will result in discord and harm to others. Of itself though, I have not seen that evil has physical power.

- **evil can do nothing physical, but it works by influencing the minds of people so that they will do its work for it.**

Evil itself can do nothing to us physically. It works on our minds. Evil can instill fear and hatred in people, and they can then choose to harm others – or themselves. I also believe that it influences other living things like birds and animals to move in certain ways - even bacteria – so that the results of their actions will harm people – but perhaps that is going too far and too fast for most people – yet!

But back to my story. When I persisted in telling our vicar that the power being released at that time by the Holy Spirit was being used in the wrong way – it was being used to exclude people rather than include them - he was quite convinced that I was possessed by evil spirits, and that is when it was decided that these spirits needed to be exorcised.. If the exorcism a group of Ministers performed on me later was supposed to drive out any evil and make me see things their way, I'm afraid it didn't do what it was intended to do. I was not "possessed" by evil in the way they believed. I had been given free will and I believed that the messages I was receiving were all from God - I was willing to obey His instructions. I had to learn the hard way about this opposing force of evil, and the Christian Church itself, as well as other religions, will need to take another look at the forces that influence them and whether they are obeying God - or evil pretending to be God - in some of the decisions they make. One of the things I had to learn for myself was how to distinguish between the ideas God was putting into my head, and the ideas evil was presenting as it pretended to be God. It was a hard lesson because it landed me in a psychiatric hospital.

After the Life in the Spirit seminar I had been learning many lessons through parables of nature. I carried a notebook around the farm with me and learned that a wise gardener would allow the weeds to grow along with the crop - for a while - but he would not allow them to smother the crop. I was woken up in the night with vivid dreams and thoughts in my head, and I had to quietly get up and write them down on scraps of paper. One night I had a vivid dream and saw the outline of a dark figure on a huge dark chair, surrounded by such a vivid light I could not bear to look at it. Then I felt three bursts as of power in my arm and a voice saying, "Is that enough?"

"Yes," I gasped, "I don't want to be greedy!" and then I was wide awake, still feeling the power in my arm. That was the only time God was ever shown to me in a form that was recognizably human.

Another night I was told, "I have healed your body. Take it and use it in my service."[4] I wondered how, and the answering vivid thought, almost a voice, said, "By writing." Shortly after this I was awakened one night by a tingling in my whole body and I had to get up and write again. This message was dictated phrase by phrase so that I did not have any idea of a sentence as a whole, but just wrote a few words at a time as they were given to me. I was to keep it until someone came for it – someone who honoured their mother and father. I thought at first that that meant a human mother and father, but later I came to believe that it meant Mother Nature and Father

---

[4] I had previously spent five weeks in a large city hospital with a heart attack.

God. No-one has really come for it yet, but this is the message that I will be passing on here for anyone who cares to listen. By this time I was beginning to accept what had happened to me, and that God was communicating with me and teaching me lessons that I would some day write down and teach other people, especially children. We would have to start with the children and be patient. My attention was drawn to pregnant women and I was told my work would be for these future generations.

One of the most vivid lessons occurred when I had been learning that our heavenly Father knows what we will need and will provide it - but we must make an effort for ourselves. God does not condone apathy or laziness. I think I had begun to take God's help for granted. I had a precious cow about to calve and I dearly wanted a heifer calf. Though the cow had had trouble calving the year before, I was sure that all would be well and God would see I got my heifer calf. One Sunday afternoon I had been feeling that I needed to go and look at something on the farm. I went obediently as I have tried to be obedient all through my experiences, and I saw that all was not quite right with the cow, but I thought, "It's too much trouble to get her in now and look at her. God will see that everything is all right." The next morning I went out expecting to see my heifer calf and found the cow in great distress. We had to get the vet, and take the calf away from her. She was in agony and I was in even greater agony of spirit. I felt as though I was seeing Christ crucified and I was partly to blame because God had shown me the signs and I had done nothing but leave it to Him. As soon as I had realized this lesson, the calf came easily and it was a bull, dead of course. As soon as I have learned a lesson, God has shown his mercy as well, because all along whatever has looked so frightening in prospect has never been so bad when faced up to.

A year later, when I had started teaching Sunday School, the lesson was repeated for me, and I have been reminded again recently that I need to repeat it for those who may read my writings.

I and my Sunday School students had been invited just down the road to visit the other village church where I had gone to Sunday School myself. Parents called to pick up their children an hour after Sunday School started and I had planned to be back in plenty of time, but an elder there was telling a story to the children and went on and on. I was worried that we wouldn't be back before the parents arrived and I was praying, "Please God, get him to stop." He did not stop and then the thought was put in my head as clear as a bell, "You do it!" I was horrified, but I had no option but to stand up in his church, interrupt him and say, "Excuse me Mr ---, but I need to take the children back. Their parents will be calling for them." It was so hard for me to do, but lessons learned like that are never forgotten. Whenever there is something that needs to be done, no matter how hard for me, if it is something I could make an effort to do, I can hear that message, "You do it.!" That is one of the messages I need to pass on to Christians or to any others who believe in a force for good in the world. Don't just pray to God to do what you know needs to be done – or for others to make a start on it. "You do it!"

Looking back, I can see that in the beginning, God had been teaching me about Himself, and what I would need to know about what He wanted. - and He was doing this before He allowed me to be fully exposed to the force of evil. I needed to experience evil for myself however, if I was going to be able to teach about it also.

Back in the year 2007, he allowed me to feel the full force of that malignancy again - just for a few seconds in a nightmare before I woke still feeling the horrible power. I think it was a reminder to me, in May 2007, that I still had not written the second part of the work that I had been given to do. I thought I had finished the first part. I had written the teaching resources about ethics for a multi-cultural society, that are based on reason and not on religion. I had battled to get acceptance in our own educational system of the ethical formula that God gave me right at the beginning of my teaching. I had opened a web-site and put God's ethical principles there for free access to anyone who is interested – to be used as a global ethic in a multi-cultural world, but I had not written yet for the ordinary people about the God I know, and the power of the force of evil. I knew I must not put it off any longer. I must not settle down comfortably in my chair in the evenings with my knitting. There is still work to be done. Another of Evil's little tricks – lulling me into apathy and carelessness.

As soon as I began to write again about the force of evil, I was under constant attack, just as I was in the beginning. I had several narrow misses in my car when my attention had been diverted by an unusual happening, and at last, success on evil's part when I grazed another car on a roundabout – I had not seen him indicate that he was going to turn in front of me. I hate that sound of metal crushing metal, and I know that evil inspires other drivers to take risks that may frighten or harm me. It put my own car out of action for several weeks. Only one of a succession of unpleasant happenings that evil was using as a warning to intimidate me and make life difficult – suggesting that these things would not have happened if I had left evil alone to get on with its work. A car nearly knocked me over on a pedestrian crossing, but God always brings good out of the bad things that evil causes to happen to us, and all this prompted me to get on with the writing that I needed to do.

The attacks have continued. The electric power connection into the house came loose, burning out many of our power appliances and leaving some alive that could have electrocuted us. If we had not been in the house it could have burnt down and I would have lost all my writings. On the way to an examination at the hospital in the city, we were sandwiched between two trucks and trailers, one merging on the left and one overtaking on the right leaving us nowhere to go because traffic was nose to tail. The driver of the truck that scraped along our side and took off the rear vision mirror was terribly upset because he had thought we would have been caught under his trailer and killed. My husband was very shaken about it but I was told in the beginning that I would need to have nerves of steel. My work is not finished yet, so whatever evil throws at us, we will survive until it is time to go. In October.2012, I walked into a bank robbery in our local town where one of the robbers had a gun. Looking back I think I must have been in real danger, because this was one of the few times since the early days that I have felt that I was under some sort of power that was guiding my actions. My intention was to find a parking space closer to the bank but I was moved to use a parking space much further up the street which meant that I reached the bank several minutes later than I would have done if I had followed my normal practice. A few minutes earlier and I would have been at the teller's window when the robbers took over. Those few minutes meant that the robbery was in process when I entered the bank. A member of the bank staff was on the floor just inside the door and managed to quietly warn me to go back outside which I finally did without the robbers noticing me. This teller was later given an award for bravery.[5] The gun could have "accidentally" gone off, but as it was I stood outside the bank door almost in a trance, watched the robbers escape through the side door of the bank and no-one was injured. In the latest episode, in February 2014, an encounter with a wasp's nest and many stings on my face nearly accomplished evil's mission for it, but God's timing had seen that help arrived in time before the swelling blocked my airways completely. A grand-daughter who is a nurse had been staying with me for a few days. She called an ambulance and the fire service arrived with oxygen well before an ambulance could reach our rural area.

Now in 2015, obviously I have still not finished my work of writing about the God I know and the force of evil. Much has happened over the last few years. There have been ups and downs of success and despair as far as my writing about God's righteousness for a modern world is concerned, but at least it is there. At first, before I learned to watch out for the different voices of God and the force pretending to be God, I kept being told, "No self! No self!" and I believed God was telling me not to write about myself, but over the years I began to wonder if I had been mistaken and it had not been God's voice. There are my diaries of course, but over the last two years I have written most of my story in such a way that others will understand about my background and the times in which I lived. These two years have also been filled with hospitals and blood transfusions for my husband, and heart problems and a pacemaker for me. The voices used to say, "Remember the blood! Remember the blood!" and at that time I understood them to be referring to Christ's blood, and that

---

[5]   Franklin County News - Police thank brave teller. P 1. 19.3. 2013

what I was finally going to have to say would be letting him down. It is not a coincidence that the problems my husband and I have had as our bodies deteriorate in our old age, have had a lot to do with blood, reminding me of those times. Was it a coincidence that my husband caught such a bad dose of hepatitis thirty years ago, that the effects on his liver caused him such trouble in his old age? Was it a coincidence that he chose to drink from the very glass that had just been handled by a carrier of the disease? I can see evil putting the thought in his head, "Choose that glass," or influencing the barman, "You're too busy. Don't bother to sterilize the glasses," - because that is how evil works.

How am I so sure about the way in which God and evil communicate with us?

I wish I had known from the start, but it was all part of the education that was given to me in the early stages of my journey. Evil was so confident then, and I was so ignorant and had so much to learn. One day there was some particular problem on my mind, I can't remember now all the details – and the thoughts were coming thick and fast, but suddenly one thought was just too fast and I had that sudden flash of knowledge when God showed me that I hadn't had time to produce that thought by myself. It had arrived in my brain fully fledged with no effort on my part. Humans have invented computers that can copy documents in a flash and send them round the world. Is it so unbelievable that a force beyond ourselves should have the same ability?

I wish I had known from the start that there were two different forces communicating with me. I would probably never have ended up in the psychiatric hospital, but I know I had to experience this for myself. It is beginning to be accepted today that some psychiatric patients really do hear voices.. Quite often they believe God is telling them to commit acts of violence. I know that evil is trying to discredit God in this way. I did hear voices in a way, as scraps of conversation seemed to be speaking directly to me, and thoughts were being put into my head, but there are still some things for which I have no explanation. Research is ongoing, but scientific researchers will need to have open minds – and they should not ignore the stories of the experiences of the prophets or people like Buddha. Look for the similarities not the differences.

3.3.'13 - God continues to lead me to items of interest.

Yesterday, in the week-end newspaper[6] there was an article telling how, by implanting electrodes in the brains of two rats, scientists now claimed to have proved that information can be transferred by brain waves. These electrodes were one hundredth the width of a human hair but when the "encoded" rat pressed a lever an electrical version of its brain activity was transferred to the "receiver" rat in another cage thousands of miles away, and 70% of the time the receiver rat performed the same action. Scientists consider 70% to be well above the level of chance – and of course 100% of the messages might have got through, but like us, a considerable proportion of the time the receiver might have chosen to ignore them.

My story from 1975 is all there of course in my diaries. My lesson plans that cover the years from 1977 to 1997 are still on my shelves, also some copies of the information I have given to various people

---

[6] Collins, N.(2013, March 2) Mind-reading a step closer. N.Z. Herald p B 7.

in authority in the church over the years. I am tempted to decide that that is enough, but if I left it at that, I would be passing the work on to others after I am dead, and I need to make it easier for them by putting it together in a simple readable form myself. I feel that there is too much for me to do, but as with all the work I have been given, once I get started it will not be as bad as I feared. Another of evil's little tricks – making us think that the job is too big and we are inadequate. Remember you are not alone. Just get started and plod along in the right direction. Looking back you will wonder how you managed it. It will be the same in the battle against evil. Someone needs to have the courage to take the first step and then God will be able to motivate people to join in and help. In one way the move is already beginning. At the end of 2009 there was a meeting at Copenhagen of leaders from all around the world recognizing that humans need to protect their environment before it is too late. In reports from the meeting it was possible to see evil working on human minds in order to prevent them from reaching agreements that would be a step in the right direction and that would enable God to help us.

In April 2012 my husband died. The damage caused to his liver had finally brought his life to an end and I must go on alone. I have good family and friends around me and now I really must do what is needed to finish my work. I believe God will give me time, but I must not waste it. Evil will undoubtedly be suggesting that I have plenty of time, but I have never been a gambler. One thing I know for sure though. I must not allow myself to get so wrapped up in this writing that I isolate myself from my friends and my everyday life. It would be too easy for evil to suggest that my mind was unsound in my later years. I was warned from the beginning, "No excess. No excess." So the middle of the road it is.

The oak tree that divided. One limb grew strong and straight.

4

FOR SUCH A TIME AS THIS

I did not know about it then of course, but now I believe that my experience of evil began in my earliest childhood. My husband complained about books with flash-backs. He was never quite sure with some, when or where the action was supposed to be taking place, but before I go any further with my story, I need to explain a bit more about my background. In the early days after 1975, I often asked, "Why me God? Why me? I didn't ask for anything really. I didn't think we should ask for gifts. All I wanted was for you to be close to me again as my friend and someone I could talk to. I did not want anything else." The reply was that I had been specially bred for the work I was going to have to do. As time went on I understood this much more clearly, and just recently, scientists have come up with new findings from research that there are inherited genes that affect the ability of people to feel mental pain. They seem to be more sensitive than others. Eventually they may discover more that will show that it is possible for some people to be more spiritually aware than others. Just recently I have been reminded several times of the story of Esther in the Old Testament of The Bible. First it was the speaker at a large local women's gathering, who took as her theme the story of Esther, and that Esther had been bred "for such a time as this." By this time of my life I was not consciously listening or watching for messages from God, but this phrase was emphasized so much that it seemed as though it was meant to get through to me. Then her story came up again at the next church service. Only time will tell if I was bred "for such a time as this."

My father's family were strong Baptists. The family records show six Job Heaths in succession, going back to the 1600s. My father, I was told, was a very religious gentle man. My brother and I were not baptised as infants, and if my father had stayed with us we would have grown up within the Baptist Church, sincerely believing all that we were taught. God always has the ability to bring good out of the harm that evil does, and so in the end, I was to benefit from the spirituality of that side of my family, but also from the colonial practicality of my mother's side. My mother's family were probably the nominal Anglicans that made up a great deal of the colonial population of New Zealand. The Ten Commandments were their ethical code. They were "upright" people and my mother was a very "upright" woman. An aunt once told me that my mother was a hard woman. If she seemed that way to other women of her time, it was probably because circumstances had forced her to be that way. She was uncompromising in her beliefs of justice and of right and wrong, and doing her duty as she saw it. I was the hybrid fruit of that union that God needed for the work he planned. I had a strong belief in God and his righteousness, but I had little knowledge of church dogma and I was not tied to the teachings of any particular Christian church.

My parents were married in 1915, and with their first little daughter, they came here around 1917, to work the farm. My father had been a self-employed builder in the city, and my mother, though she had been brought up in the country, had moved to the city during World War 1, to become a book-keeper at a large grocery wholesaler. She boarded with my father's family, and so the two were brought together. My religious father could have been a conscientious objector, but after they were married, my practical mother persuaded him to move to the farm, so that as a married man with a child and in essential work, he would not be conscripted. This preyed on his conscience, and as the wounded and gassed men came home after the war, it was even worse for him. He had stayed behind in safety - but he could not have brought himself to kill other men. His favourite sister died in the 1918 flu' epidemic, and then when their beloved daughter of two years of age also died of the flu, the whole situation preyed on his mind even more. I can see evil at work, prompting his thoughts. He should have gone to serve King George in some way. These deaths were a punishment to him for escaping to the country instead of going off to fight like the others. He had times of severe depression, and nothing seemed to help.

My brother was born in 1922 and the next year my mother's father died. He was a man ahead of his time in that he left his two daughters equal shares of his estate with his four sons. His action was not based on any ideological theory, but on events in his own family. His father, one of the earliest settlers of Auckland[7], had died when his children were young, and in his will he had ensured that his young daughters

---

[7]   He was master of a sailing ship in and out of New Zealand from 1833. In 1843 he sold his barque to Logan and Brown and bought his farm at Epsom – a farm that many years later became Alexandra Park.

would be provided for in such a way that their future husbands would have no control of their inheritance. The husband of my grandfather's elder daughter had died leaving her with three children and no bread-winner. The mental health of his second daughter's husband was precarious and she had a baby son. His grand-children were precious to him. He was terminally ill and his daughters were closer to him than his son's wives. His sons would be able to provide for their own children, but he saw that his daughters would need all the help he could give them.

My mother sent my father on a holiday to Australia with his brother for company in an effort to improve his health, but to no avail. I was born in 1924 to the great joy of everyone. At last another daughter to make up for the one that was lost – but the joy was not to last. My father still had times when he wanted to go to be with God and with his sister and his first little daughter – but he wanted the rest of his little family to go with him. My mother never told us what it was that finally pushed the family to have my father committed to the city's Mental Asylum. Only in my seventies was I accidentally let know by the son of one of my mother's neighbours. It seems that my mother had seen him go into the baby's room. She followed him to check on him and found him with a pillow over my face. She immediately contacted his family, told them that she couldn't bring herself to do it, but they would have to have him committed to a mental institution.

So the next part of our lives began. Looking back with the knowledge that I have now, I can see how evil worked on my father's mind, putting suggestions into his head, just as it does with many such sensitive people today. The difference is that mind-dulling drugs are used now to prevent the messages getting through. If such people do not take their medication they are vulnerable to evil. In my father's day of the 1920s, people were just committed to institutions and rarely came out – unless they escaped. Looking back at my life now, and seeing all the reasons that are given for psychological disturbances in children, sometimes I find it strange that I am reasonably normal. At least I consider I am fairly well-balanced. I think children can survive most things as long as they have some-one in their lives they can trust to be completely reliable. Our mother was the rock for us. And at that time so many people had been affected by World War 1, and the misery during the Depression years, that there was hardship all around us. People were expected to "just get on with it."

Some of my earliest real memories are of sleeping in a large double bed with my mother, I on one side of her, my brother on the other and a shot-gun under her pillow. At night the house was booby-trapped with chairs turned over and placed in strategic positions. We just accepted the situation as normal for us. If we thought about it at all, possibly I think we may have believed it was because we lived out in the country, and at that time of the great depression of the 1930s, there were many "swaggies" who called around looking for a meal, some work and a place to sleep. We also had men working for my mother and these men slept in a room off the back of the house. My mother worked with them clearing the land, and never left the house with us children without her shot-gun. She always said it was to shoot rabbits, and we often had stewed rabbit for dinner, but I knew later that if my father had escaped and had come to take us all with him to a "better" place, she would have been prepared to use the gun on him – even though she loved him. I had my first lessons in obedience and self-control out on the farm. I learned as a very small infant not to stray off the rug on which she placed me. At first she would surround the rug with gorse prickles so that I learned what the word "prickles" meant. As I got a bit older her croquet friends were amazed that all she had to do was place me on a rug, say "prickles," and I would stay happily on the rug playing with my toys.

Though I do not remember being concerned about it at the time, I was a solitary child with few friends outside school hours. We did not socialize much outside the family either. Maybe it was because we lived three miles outside the village, but looking back to those times, I can see that there was a social stigma attached to having a family member in a mental hospital. My mother learned a few years later that some of my father's family had told people he was dead rather than admit to his whereabouts. There was also a social stigma attached later to being divorced. In the eyes of many in society, my mother should have been ashamed of herself, but instead, she had her own farm where she employed at least three men. She was one of the first women in the district to own and drive her own car - and she had complete control of her time and her income. I think there may have been a little envy from other women around, but I know that I grew up rather socially inadequate.

Sadly, my only memory of my father was of visiting him in the old Mental Asylum in the city. It was closed long ago. That visit certainly left a psychological scar on me, as well as a physical scar, and probably led to my horror of mental institutions that was only cured by my own experience of being a patient in one. I remembered a pleasant man who peeled an orange while keeping the peel in his hand and giving my brother and I segments to eat. It was after the visit with him that the trauma occurred. My mother had driven the thirty miles north in the 1924 Buick car she had bought and learned to drive after her father's death. She had parked in the grounds but we were going on a few miles further north to see my father's brother, so on getting back to the car, my mother asked a gardener if there was a different way out of the grounds that would lead on to the main road north. The gardener directed us through a large gate, but on passing through the gate we found ourselves in an area surrounded by buildings with verandahs on the first floors, and on these verandahs were what seemed to be hundreds of deranged people, all jumping around, waving arms and shouting and screaming at us. My mother frantically backed out of the compound as fast as she could and got the car out on to the main road. I could never remember why, but we stopped shortly afterwards for my mother to check on my brother in the back seat, and when we got back into the car, my mother was obviously so upset she was not fully aware of what she was doing and slammed the car door on my finger, the end of which was squashed flat. It is still out of shape as an occasional reminder.

I often wonder whether my mother married my step-father, partly as protection, as we grew too old to sleep in her bed. As I said before, God is able to bring good out of the bad things that happen to us. A few bad things happened, but my step-father, as a Roman Catholic, added to my education in the field of main-stream religion. I was warned that no-one was to be criticized or condemned, but the truth had to be told. My step-father was the product of the things that had happened to him. He had been born in the gold-fields of Ballarat. He had been brought up by Roman Catholic nuns, but when he was due for an old-age pension here in New Zealand when he reached the age of 60, we could not trace a birth certificate, and my mother's brother had to sign a statement saying he had known my step-father since he came here in the 1930s. He had told us that he had a brother in Australia, but we could not trace him either. Before they married my mother had paid for him to have a trip back to Australia for the opening of the Sydney Harbour bridge. Perhaps it was also for him to decide if he really wanted to stay here. My mother had to be divorced so that they could marry. The Anglican Church would not marry them. The Catholic Church would not marry them, so in the end they were married at a ceremony performed by "Uncle Tom" at the radio station called "The Friendly Road." My step-father was good to my mother in their old age and they are both long dead, so I need only explain about how he contributed to my experience of organized religion and my personal understanding of God.

All of these experiences were my training to make me ready for the work God had planned for me. I had written on one of the notes in my folder, "A knowledge of nature is essential for a proper understanding of God." I can accept that I was chosen for this work because my life would keep me close to nature and I would spend a great deal of time alone with nature, enabling God to lead my thoughts along lines that would take me to what He wanted me to see. It is not easy for people in cities to be alone or quiet, though God has shown me some of his parables when I have been in cities.

I had a strong belief in God, and in the teachings of Jesus as a way of life, but I did not have an absolute belief in the teachings of the organized church. When the charismatic movement caused such a turmoil in the church here, one of our members said that she had always seen the minister and the church as the authorities and the liaison between her and God. Now she realized that she could have a personal line to God that did not depend on minister or church.

The organized church had never been part of my personal relationship with God, so I had an open mind when the charismatic movement came to town, and when my more intimate experiences with God – and evil – began. My simple education at Sunday School, and the basic Christianity I had learned there and at secondary school, made me question some of the teaching of this new movement. Jesus had said, "Judge not lest ye be judged," but some of these enthusiastic people were judging others in the church. One elderly wonderful kind member of the congregation was told sadly by one of the initiated that she wasn't a Christian because she hadn't been "born again." One thing I did see clearly was that within the Charismatic movement as it was shown to us, the God I knew seemed to have disappeared from the scene as far as the teaching was concerned.. Everyone now seemed to be worshipping Jesus, rather than a God who cared for all people. It was only later that I realized evil was pretending to be God, narrowing the thinking of the new movement into concentrating on Jesus, and sometimes turning people against each other. That was the last message I gave to our minister before we left for overseas after my experiences in the mental hospital.

It was only years later when I began my studies of world religions that I realized how important the position of Jesus is to the possibility of religions coming together - to the concept of God – the force for good in the world – and as an umbrella over all mankind. One of my instructions was not to get involved in useless theological arguments, and I still don't quite understand the doctrine of the Trinity. I am not alone in this however, because one of our church leaders told us about his father who went to a different church in London every Trinity Sunday to see how different ministers would explain it. If Christians continue to hold to the doctrine of the Trinity, a teaching that seems to claim Jesus to be an integral part of God, then the people of the Book - Jews, Christians and Muslims - whose history all goes back to Abraham, will never unite against evil.

This example from an authoritative book on world religions shows how important this is.

"The most important article in Muslim theology is 'There is no god but God.' No statement about God seemed to Muhammad more fundamental than the declaration that God is one, and no sin seemed to him so unpardonable as associating another being with God on terms of equality."[8] Divide and conquer is evil's plan.

I like this poem By James Leigh Hunt (1784-1869)

I think I must have learned it at secondary school and it has stayed with me all my life. It may help other people to understand the God I know. .

Abou Ben Adhem

Abou Ben Adhem (may his tribe increase)
Awoke one night from a deep dream of peace
And saw within the moonlight in his room
An angel writing in a book of gold.
Exceeding peace had made Ben Adhem bold
And to the creature in the room he said,
"What writest thou?" The vision raised its head,
And with a look made all of sweet accord,
Answered, "The names of those who love the Lord."

---

[8] Noss D. and Noss J. (1994) *A history of the world's religions.* (9th edition) pp 591- 2 U.S. MacMillan College Publishing Co.

"And is mine one?" said Abou. "Nay, Not so."

Replied the angel. Abou spoke more low

But cheerily still; and said, "I pray thee then,

Write me as one who loves his fellow men." The angel wrote and vanished.

The next night It came again with a great wakening light,

And showed the names whom love of God had blessed,

And Lo! Ben Adhem's name led all the rest.

So much of the teaching of Jesus as recorded in the New Testament of the Bible is focused around concern for other people and treating them as we ourselves would like to be treated, regardless of race, religion or position in life. For example in Chapter 25 verse 40 of the Book of Matthew where the people are told. "and the King will answer them, "Truly I say to you, as you did it to one of the least of these my brothers, you did it to me." (ESV)

5

MORE EXPERIENCE WITH EVIL

B ut back now to my experiences after my report to the Vestry (and these could be interesting to those who deal with mental illness today.) I can't be quite sure now how many months went by as I continued my lessons, but then everything seemed to happen at once. I did not know then that God had been protecting me from evil, but that finally He would have to remove his protection so that I could understand for myself how evil works. Suddenly I seemed to be being groomed for some part for which I was not really right. I had to put my house in order. I knew that partly it was the house of my own heart, but all around me forces were telling me it was my home and everything had to be spotless. I had too many clothes, too many shoes, too little time to do the things I should be doing for God. Messages came - by jumping out of the newspaper, or phrases from the television, or peoples' conversation. There were scriptural references to look up for instruction, but my knowledge of the Bible wasn't good enough. One voice kept saying, "Remember the blood! Remember the blood!" I wasn't to go north. I wasn't to trust anything from the East, and I was desperately trying to follow all the instructions being given to me because I thought they were all from God. I was shown that the minah birds stood for evil spirits, and that when the bulls were roaring there was danger.

One message that made me send my husband on a special trip to the Inland Revenue Department was that I owed $729.00. Later I realized that it was not the Inland Revenue Dept that I owed, but the Church or God. In our materialistic world, however, fear that I might have underpaid taxes took precedence over any guilt that I might have underpaid God. In the following years I learned that guilt played a large part in the power that evil can exercise over people. It is not that we should not feel guilty at all over things we have done that have harmed other people. If we feel no guilt we will not make any effort to improve our actions. A little guilt is a good thing if it inspires us to put things right and improve our behaviour in the future. As Aristotle taught, the middle way is best. Excess guilt is what is harmful and excess guilt is what evil can work on, and is what makes us vulnerable to Evil's attacks. Excess guilt may have been taught by the Christian Church as the force of evil pretended to be God. Part of my training had been, "No excess! No excess!"

Though I didn't realize it at the time, I was receiving messages from both God and evil. I did not realize then that it was up to me to sort out which messages came from which force. By the time God had released me from my exposure to the power of evil, I had learned to distinguish the difference. It must have been at this time that I learned about the ways God communicates with us by putting thoughts in our heads, and finally to distinguish the difference between the communications of God and the force of evil as it was pretending to be God – and the most important point - that we have free will, and what we do with those thoughts is then up to us. As I told my friend's husband, we choose whether we will listen to God or evil.

That is how I came to learn the principles which are the basis of the ethical formula that was given to me. God will always want us to use the reason we have been given and consider the long-term consequences of our actions, but Evil will offer us immediate attractive rewards. Temptation is its weapon. God will never ask us to do anything that will injure any other person, but evil will try to convince us that the end will justify the means. God will expect us to treat people justly and not to favour one over another without good cause, whereas evil will present many reasons for doing just that, especially if treating some people with what appears at first sight to be justice, results in being unjust to others, and arouses more resentment in them. God will never suggest we should lie or deceive other people, but evil delights in deception, and especially deception that it can use to cause trouble between people, then or at some later date.

Experience is the best teacher, and being allowed to experience for myself the way evil works was necessary, and though unpleasant at the time, I do not think it has harmed me. I was so frightened of evil at first, but I was told that I would need nerves of steel if I was to accomplish my task and that it was all part of my training. Several years later, I wrote, "You would have thought I would have learned by now that the voice that speaks urgently in my ear, demanding actions is not God. God shows me his messages by things that are true in the world of nature around me, and I believe the messages that come in the night when my mind is empty of other things are from God. It will be up to others to decide the truth of that, but Nature does not lie."

It seems to me now that the further we get from nature in our modern lives, the more likely it is that we can be deceived by the blandishments of evil.

The messages kept coming, At this time I believed it was only God who was communicating with me, and I was trying to obey and do what ever I was told to do. I was rushing around trying to straighten out everything in my life and home that I was being told was not right with God. While I was frantically trying to obey and clean up my house I was shown that in my folder where I had put all my writings, I had written a few things that, if they were examined, might have hurt other people. I tried to find them and take the pages out, but I could never find what I wanted. In the end I had it impressed on me that the best thing to do was to burn the lot, which I did, and of course burnt much of the evidence of the references and messages I had been given up till then. The final blow came when I found in our garage some chemical material that had been given to me for use on the farm. I thought perhaps the person who had given it to me had taken it from his place of work without permission as a "perk." Guilt over this gave evil the chance to drive me to desperation. The police would come and find it. The person who gave it to me would be in serious trouble and perhaps lose his job. Because I was an official in the church, it would be a disgrace to God's name. In desperation I tried to get rid of the material, but it was bright yellow in colour and wherever I went the colour yellow seemed to leap out at me reminding me of my guilt. Cars, flowers, A.A. signs – my attention was drawn to anything yellow to keep reminding me of how guilty I was, and how I had let God down because I wasn't fit to do his work. No wonder my family thought I was acting very strangely, but through it all I believed sincerely that I was obeying God and that I was being asked to do a specific work for Him. I didn't have to do it. I could have opted out, but it was for the sake of Jesus Christ and all the children to come. Also for my parents to make up for all they had suffered.

The night after I tried to get rid of the yellow material, some children were staying with us for the night. The little boy had suffered from asthma attacks, and the knowledge was put into my mind that the evil forces were getting at me through him, and trying to intimidate me into giving up the work I had to do. An older child came in to us in the early hours of the morning and said the boy was having an asthma attack. It was a bad attack and there was nothing we could do, but I was told I had to pray for him or he would die. I had never prayed in front of my family and I was embarrassed, but did as I was told, praying silently to myself. Then I was told to pray aloud which I did, though I hated making an exhibition of myself as I saw it. While I was holding his head and praying he was quiet. I was sure I was receiving God's help to protect him. Whenever I stopped praying aloud he would start to cough again and the voice speaking to me in my head said "Keep praying." Finally his parents came to get him, but I was told he still wasn't safe and to keep praying and the voice said "Louder! Louder!"

Looking back later I realized that the voice I was obeying was not God's voice, though it was deceiving me into believing it was God. I realized later also how easy it is to be deceived into thinking we are doing what God wants when it is really the force of evil we are hearing. I was very handicapped in my reasoning at the time, because I had never really believed there was a Satan or force for evil. Anyway, I had been told by people in the church that the name of "Jesus Christ" was more powerful than evil. All you have to do, they said, is to invoke the name of Jesus Christ and evil will be vanquished. It would be nice if it were as easy as that. When I was asked to do things I did not want to do, I would ask, "In the name of Jesus Christ do I really have to do that?" and the answer would be "Yes." - and I would do it in spite of my natural reluctance. I wanted to obey God.

As far as I was concerned at the time, evil spirits just did not enter my thinking. To come to see that evil is an active force that actively draws the eye and ear to what it wants you to see is a frightening thing. I kept having my attention drawn to knives, but I never accepted suicide as a way out of the difficulties of my tasks. I can see now how psychiatric patients are influenced by the force of evil and why they often believe God has been asking them to do the things they do. I believe also that is how so many accidents happen. Evil distracts our attention momentarily by drawing it to something else, and in that split second something happens that could have been avoided if we had not been drawn to seeing or listening to something else. My husband often complained that he had had traffic tickets for comparatively harmless misdemeanors, while he saw other drivers doing far more dangerous things on the roads and they didn't seem to get caught. My own belief is that such people are not caught at first, because evil has plans for them to carry on and do a great deal more damage, but of course I could not tell my husband that. He had suffered enough already and I think he thought I had got over all that. I never told him about the exorcism either, because he would have been very annoyed with the church – and worried that I had consented to it. We did not talk about such things after I was released from the psychiatric hospital, and I did not want to upset him, or make him wonder if I really had been cured. There must always have been a worry in his mind that insanity might really be hereditary. Now that he is no longer alive, I can tell more of my story.

At that time I believed that God was telling me I had to keep praying for the child or he would die, and I believed it was God who was telling me to pray "Louder. Louder." It shows how we can be so convinced that God is speaking to us, that we can lose all our sense of reason. Religions need to take another look at themselves now. God told me later to stop looking for signs and messages. He had given me wisdom and I was to use it. God has given mankind large brains, but they also need open minds. History tells us that during the "Enlightenment" of the nineteenth century many of the best brains of the time rejected the teachings of the Christian Church. The Church needs those best brains today to make new wine for the new bottles of the educated masses. Perhaps my story will reach some of them.

If I were to give all the details of what happened to me in the next few months this book would be far too long, but my husband called a doctor that night because I would not stop praying loudly, and when an Indian doctor came in answer to the call, it was the last straw for me. I had been told not to trust anyone from the East and I had been expecting our family doctor who I was sure would understand when I explained to him. This new doctor gave me an injection and in the morning, after an ambulance ride I found myself in a psychiatric hospital, still in full possession of my wits as far as I was concerned, and still obeying to the best of my ability what I regarded as instructions from God.

After I was admitted there, I believed I was still perfectly clear in my mind, but still willing to obey. I was persuaded by my vivid thoughts or voices that I had to try and stay in my dressing gown for a few days, and in that time I was asked to do several things to draw attention to myself. Firstly I had to kneel for half an hour on the stones at the foot of the steps in the drizzling rain until the staff made me go inside. I was to pray aloud in the lounge, at my bedside until stopped, and finally pray in the toilet until stopped. I hated doing these things, and it was typical of evil's cruelty to make me do things that were so difficult and embarrassing for me, but I did them because I believed God was requesting it. I had believed the members of the church when they said that if we asked something "in the name of Jesus Christ" it would be answered. I had a great deal to learn.

Sometimes there were gentler instructions that I had no problem in obeying. There was a crippled girl, and one day I was asked to rub her legs and pray quietly for her. There was a poor man who couldn't control his muscles and I was asked to sit by him and help him. We played charades – the name of a song - and I had to put my arms around him and have him hold on to me as we acted "Rock of Ages." Looking back over the years I often wondered what had happened to them. Had my actions helped them in any way?

I was also wakened now and again at night by this tingling all over my body and told to pray for unknown people who needed it, and several times to get up and write what I remembered of the first letter which had been dictated to me, and which I had been told to ask my husband to destroy when I was admitted to the hospital. I am sure now that it was evil that insisted on that letter being destroyed. Several of the letters I wrote at that time I was told to keep because someone was going to come for them, but no-one did, and I was then told to destroy them. They may have been undecipherable, because when I got home, I found a sheet of paper with my writing on it and it was quite disjointed. I had had trouble writing the correct references at times, as though some force was deliberately trying to make me make mistakes. It is amazing how the force of evil can distort our hearing, our vision and even our memory to make us believe that what we are doing is right and is God's will. I have always since had to check and recheck what I have read and written. Much of what I am writing now is coming directly from the account I wrote after I was allowed to leave the psychiatric hospital and return to my normal life. I was shown then that I had to keep a written record of events so that as time passed, memories of what had happened could not be distorted.

6

THE PSYCHIATRIC HOSPITAL

People have recently been making claims of cruelty in the psychiatric hospitals of that era. I do not remember that the staff were deliberately cruel, but they had a job to do, and they were doing what they considered most beneficial and practical for the patients at the time. Later my husband and I were some of those who protested against the closing of that psychiatric hospital and the waste of all the buildings there. It was a far more pleasant environment than the mental hospital I had seen in the city when I was a child. I will never be suing the government because of the way I was treated there. I know I must have been very exasperating to the staff. I refused to take the pills I was supposed to take - because I was being told by these vivid thoughts or voices not to take drugs. When my behaviour did not seem to be improving as far as the staff were concerned, I was taken one day into a small room and, surrounded by several male and female nurses, given a choice. Either I took the pills or they would give me medication by an injection. I refused the pills again and without protest was given an injection in the leg that was extremely painful. For a while longer my medication always came by injection, but I bear no ill-will towards the staff of the hospital. I was perfectly capable of making a choice. Fortunately no one ever suggested electric shock treatment. I can thank God for that because I would probably have accepted it.

The voices I heard in my head allowed me to eat very little, and drink only a little cold water each day. I believe I became dehydrated, my mouth was very dry and my saliva became salty so that my lips became encrusted with salt. I had believed at first that I was being groomed to play the part of a special messenger. I gradually moved down in status until one night when I decided that my final part was to be that of a pitiful creature crouched in the corner of a bare room, praying in a foreign tongue. It happened like this. I had been asked by my voices to pray at my bedside in tongues. When another patient complained, I was locked in a cell with a mattress on the floor and a bucket in the corner. The voices required me to keep praying, and as I became exhausted with kneeling straight up, my back would sag and a voice would command me to straighten my back. Another gentler voice kept telling me to keep my eyes on the cross in the sky and I could see a narrow cross, which looking back may have been the bars of a small window against the moonlight. When I fixed my eyes on the cross, I could find the strength to straighten my back. I was convinced I had to obey for the sake of Jesus Christ and all the children to come. We had come so far, I was not going to give in, and if I had to be this pitiful creature to make sure the message was accepted, then I was willing to carry on.

Later in the same year I wrote,

"In this manner I learned that by keeping one's eye on the cross, the things which are beyond our own strength can be accomplished. When I became too weak to kneel alone, I was allowed to hold on to the cornerstone, and when I thought the whole night must have passed, I was shown that it was only several hours, and a picture was flashed into my mind of how long it must have seemed to Jesus to have been hanging on the cross."

The part that evil plays in the symptoms and treatment of depression and psychiatric disorders should never be underestimated. My attention was constantly being drawn to anything that could upset me, for instance the colour yellow and its relationship to guilt for me. I was constantly being prompted to do things I would not normally have done. Two years later I wrote the following piece -

Evil and its fight for our minds.

"I have been reading a book by a well-known religious writer in which she talks about the way in which disaster after disaster piles up on a person and she is wondering why a loving God allows this to happen.

I don't know if I have written about how evil kept drawing my attention to knives, heaping trial upon trial on me, and then presenting me or rather drawing my attention to a knife and suggesting there was an easy way out. How much evil would have liked me to take him up on his suggestion. This is how he works, leaving us alone for a while and then heaping difficulty upon difficulty on us in rapid succession in an attempt to break us down. How he would love to see me cry. There is nothing wrong with a pride that will not allow him that satisfaction.

67

While I was in the psychiatric hospital, I saw the results of his efforts – a girl with rope burns on her neck. I am sure evil had led her beneath the same rafter many times a day in the course of her work at home, and had drawn her eyes upwards each time and made the suggestion, 'Wouldn't it be easier to end it all?' We are fighting an active force that draws our eyes forcibly to the temptations to which it wishes us to succumb. It puts thoughts in our minds that are not of our own making, and then of course, if they are thoughts we know we should resist, he delights in making us feel guilty for having such thoughts.

I can see people who are depressed being constantly reminded by things they see or hear of their own problems, and negative thoughts constantly being put into their heads. I can see people constantly being reminded of how they are being victimised by others – even incited to violence – 'You need to get your own back on them.' All sorts of possible means of revenge – even using the name of God. 'You will be helping God if you harm these people.'

Evil loves to influence people to harm others, and it loves to add fuel to arguments and dissension between people. It shovels on extra ideas, keeping the mind fixed on our own victimisation and trying to keep out reasonable argument. We do not need to fear that evil has physical power. It does not make things go bump in the night, but it could influence someone to leave a window open when it should have been shut, and then work on our minds, making suggestions about the sounds we hear, trying to influence or frighten us. If we know how it works, we can defeat it. How often I have realized its influence when my husband has thought one way and I have thought another. Because

I know how evil is trying to incite a major difference of opinion and split us up, I have gone all out to see that it doesn't succeed - though not always successfully. Patience is not one of my major virtues, but knowing how evil works helps in the battle. We need to use the qualities God offers us, courage, determination, long-suffering, wisdom, justice, truth and love."

It is easy enough to see the work of evil in the thoughts and actions of terrorists, or movements that are fuelled by hatred of other people, nations or religions, but it is not so obvious in our ordinary lives. People who suffer from depression should not spend too much time on their own where they are able to let these thoughts occupy their minds. They need to keep busy, and particularly helping those who are worse off than themselves.

When I worked on the phone for Lifeline some years later, I could see how valuable it was for people to be able to let off steam by talking to others, but I could also see that those they talked to needed to be careful that they did not add fuel to the fire. I also recognized voices of those who rang again and again without being prepared to make any effort to change their attitudes or circumstances. I often thought of the girl with rope-burns on her neck. She left the psychiatric hospital before I did. Was she going home to the same conditions that had sent her there or was she going to be able to either change her circumstances or change her attitude to them. At least by the time I left the hospital I knew what was causing my problem, and usually knew how to distinguish between the voices of good and evil. I had also learned not to worry about making mistakes. As long as I did the best I could, God was able to take any mistakes I made and bring something good out of them.

Now, when I read over the accounts of my experiences as I interpreted them at the time, I can see how my knowledge of God broadened from the background of the person I was at the time, to the person I became as I learned more and more about God and Evil and how they operate. I had a lot to learn, but at that time I thought I was only obeying God and I believed what I had been told by the church members, that if I asked "in the name of Jesus Christ," I could trust the answer. I did not know then that there was a force that was pretending to be God and that was deceiving His followers and delighting in causing dissent in the world. It is not going to be easy to convince His faithful followers of this. I am sad to think of how my good friends in the established Christian Church will regard me, and the things I am going to have to write.

7

HOME AGAIN

My time in the psychiatric hospital ended after I heard a discussion, with several voices deciding that they would have to give up their efforts to get the message through at the moment as they did not want to take a corpse out of there. They said, "Go home, live quietly, have your holiday and then we'll see." I took my pills without protest and I was discharged from the hospital two weeks later. I had a short holiday with a friend who wanted some company, and lived quietly for a week or two as I regained my strength. After a while I stopped taking the pills – which upset my husband – but I knew I did not need them[9] – and I began to feel part of the normal world again. Then one day I saw an advertisement in the daily paper from some new sect that was using the name of Jesus Christ, but was saying that we should stop trying to load the responsibility of our sins on to Jesus, accept them ourselves and live a life filled with

---

[9]   There may be plenty of people today who, on reading my story, will consider that I still need them

love and light. It seemed so reasonable and I could see how it could appeal to young people, but somehow I felt uncomfortable about it. A short while later a voice from the T.V. drew my attention to the words, "That upset you, didn't it. You will see later on tonight."

I had been sleeping badly again and each night I had gone out to the kitchen about midnight and had seen the light on the top of the hill which was comforting, and reminded me of the "light of the world." When I was awoken that night and I looked out the window there was a terrible blackness. The light was out on the hill and it flashed into my mind what was wrong with just depending on ourselves. These people were right in saying that we shouldn't load the responsibility for our sins on to Jesus. For thousands of years people have not been able to make a better world in their own strength, and for the last two thousand years, loading them on to Jesus has not made the world a much better place either. Certainly there have been advances in science and technology that have made our health better and our living conditions better – in some places - but in the process what have we been doing to our environment? And in other places science has invented better ways of blowing each other up. Have we not had enough of wars? But it is happening all over the world – leaders who can't resist the promptings of evil. "You've got your rights. Fight to see the others don't have more rights than you!. What does it matter if a few people get hurt." Look at the Middle East and you will see God being used as an excuse for a power struggle. Many people blame religion, but if we took God away, evil would suggest other reasons for fighting. Suppressing religion in Communist countries didn't make them perfect.

Removing God from the equation takes away hope. Without hope we have no incentive to try. The advertisement was partly right. It is not a matter of loading our sins on to Jesus, but of knowing that though few of us are going to be perfect, we are not alone in the fight against evil. Once we begin to make a conscious effort to fight against evil, God will help us – and we will win – but God gave us free will and we must make the first step. I only hope we don't leave it too late to make a move.

I continued to be woken in the night with short messages clear in my mind. I accepted this as part of the things I had to learn and always got out of bed and wrote them down on scraps of paper. One night I was again reminded of the 729 that was still owing. The $729 that had been given to the Inland Revenue Department had gone towards paying our taxes. 729 flashed insistently in my head and I felt that in some way it was owed to the church, so now I wrote a cheque for another $729 and gave it to the church. A few days after this I received the knowledge that it was time that I went back to the church and told our leader about the message I had had dictated to me but had asked my husband to destroy. When he asked me for whom the message had been meant, the words, "For all Christians," came out of my mouth though I had never consciously thought about it before. The charismatic movement had been supposed to be all about joy and gifts, but after my first experience there was no joy now for me, and why should anyone believe me? – After all, who was I? I was only a farmer and a housewife and I had been a patient in a psychiatric hospital.

The day I was to go back to the psychiatric hospital for a final clearance, I found I had mistaken the date, though I had looked at it many times, and I was frightened again to realize how Evil can confuse our eyes and ears. We must check and recheck, go back to the source documents. Never assume we know or remember correctly without checking. I had to wait another week and it seemed that evil was going to go all out to see that I was readmitted to the hospital and my story discredited. The minah birds, the bulls, the twin lights, the creaking doors, the aching feet and everything bright yellow – all leapt forward at me again, forcing my recognition against my will. After one terrible night I realized I needed all the help I could get. If I kept insisting on my story about the letter people would think I was mad, but if I didn't carry through with what I had been entrusted, then guilt would also send me mad, so I decided I might as well go down fighting for the message.

I realized that my pride and self-sufficiency were my weaknesses, even though I had written, "Pride is the cardinal sin," so though I always hated doing so, I went to our vicar, admitted this and asked him to ask his prayer group to pray for me. He and his wife prayed for me, asked forgiveness for me and that God would grant me His peace. I had been reading the Bible at random and there was always a message for me. One day the name Josiah caught my eye because one of my father's names was Josiah, so I read the book in which it was mentioned, and when I reached the end I found I had reached the book of Malachi - and the number of the page in my Living Bible[10] was 729. I remembered that I had written "Malachi" down somewhere as something I needed to read, and as so often had happened, the meaning jumped clearly out at me. Firstly that I had

---

[10] The Living Bible – Paraphrased – Tyyndale House Publishers, Wheaton, Illinois. 21st Printing May 1973

not been fit to deliver a message for God before this time. The dross needed to be burned away, and secondly, that God demanded that the teachers used in his service must be the very best and must honestly teach God's word. I had been told by one of our church leaders that if there was a message from God, it would be scriptural and as far as I was concerned Malachi was the confirmation of the message. Once I had handed over the whole message as I knew it, then I would have done my part, but the book of Malachi reprimands Priests who do not teach God's words correctly – and I had to take this message, very reluctantly, to the church.

By now however, I was beginning to realize and accept what was happening to me, what was being asked of me, but also that I was going to be given the strength to do it. The master craftsman can take an inadequate tool and produce the article he intends. I was the inadequate tool, but if I allowed myself to be used in the way He intended, then sooner or later the task could be accomplished. Later, however may turn out to be after I am dead, but that may be the best thing for me. Much as I want to accomplish the task I have been set, and much as I want to see results from the years of work I have done, I know that I might become the victim of PRIDE. I might be tempted to say things that could be interpreted in a wrong way. Evil would certainly be going all out to discredit me and would be pretending to be God in the process. I would be the scarlet woman of the Bible, working to discredit Jesus – suggesting he was not what the Christian religion claims him to be.

I had been told, "I have given you wisdom. Take it and use it in My service," and though I do not have a lot of confidence in myself, I know that if I make a mistake, God will take it and bring something good out of it, so I carry on, knowing my inadequacies, but doing my best.

Amazing how God works. I had refused to ask for any gifts, but I had had this little thought to myself at the time, that if I had been going to ask for any gift it would have been the gift of wisdom. I do not see myself as particularly wise, but I do see that the experiences I have had in my life along the paths in which I have been led, have given me a broad experience of people, and an understanding of how they think and act. When I married I had believed our lives were to be on the farm, living quietly in the country and doing the work I loved, but instead the path changed and we found ourselves working on wages, building a house, living in the village and then starting a business, training apprentices, doing office work, and then back to my own farm, and teaching and working with people in ways I had never imagined. God had been giving me the experiences I needed for the work He had planned for me to do, and now He had extended my education into the spiritual world.

One of the flashes of knowledge I was given at the time told me that I would be like Moses – being given a glimpse of the promised land, but others would take the people there. I have no doubt Evil will still be trying to suppress my writings -. may even put the thought into my family's heads after my death that a large rubbish skip would be the best place for them. I have to make sure that somehow my writings have been saved until they are needed.

8

BACK TO THE REAL WORLD

This was the beginning of a life that had two sides to it. I needed to live a normal life in my community. I was still being woken up during the night to write down things that had been made clear to my mind when it was free of the distractions of normal life. I was still being shown parables when the right situations presented themselves, but above all I needed to convince my husband that I was mentally stable. He had suffered enough through the first part of my experiences. Fortunately he was a heavy sleeper and never woke till it was time for him to get up in the morning. We decided to take a three month holiday, away from farm and business, and travel to Britain and Europe, joining our eldest daughter and her husband in a camper van and tent through Britain, Norway and Sweden for two months, and then leaving them at Amsterdam, going off on our own down the Rhine, and then with eurail passes and a small bag each, travelling all over Europe and finally home through the United States.

I wrote the piece that follows after this trip, and though I have looked through many folders I have not been able to find a date for it. My largest folder - a student's arch file - is daunting. It contains all the pieces of paper I used to write down the things that were shown to me, from 1975 to 1978 and some from a few years later – except of course the writings from the early days that I was persuaded to destroy. The pile of writings is at least two inches (5 cm.) thick and the edges are yellowed with age. I started the diaries in 1977, one just a straight diary and one for messages. They were foolscap size so naturally I couldn't carry them around with me and was still writing on scraps of paper, or small pads that would fit in my pocket. In looking through my old file now, my attention has been drawn several times to where I had written that I believed I could trust the things that I was shown through nature – that the things of God are simple, and that I believed I could trust the messages that came in the night.

This account describes what I learned on our trip to England and Europe and it stops with our return.

"After I had given the rest of the message over to the church, I was finally conscious of belonging completely to the world again. Right from the start, after my experience of the Blessing of the Holy Spirit, I had felt myself to be in this world, but also surrounded by a power that was beyond my understanding. Looking back now, after taking much more interest in Biblical accounts of people like the prophets and their encounters with God, the phrase, "The Holy Spirit came upon him," seems relevant here. Those who believe that the prophets were only wise men who had worked things out for themselves should go back and study the accounts of the experiences of the prophets.[11]

---

[11] For example Isaiah Chapter 10 verse 4 ESV. "Morning by morning he awakens my ear ---"

The Holy Spirit had come upon me and had been with me strongly throughout all these experiences, but now I was to be allowed to return to a more normal situation with my human reason in control. I began to feel that I had to write the whole story down – and the messages continued, the first being, "Now compulsion has gone, reason remains and the desire to write." As I wrote about all these events, over a period of a week or more, I was still woken at nights with vivid thoughts in my head that were not my own thinking, and that I had to get up and write down. I could not rely on remembering them in the morning, and over the many years that have followed, this has continued. Not so frequent once I had learned much of what I needed to learn, very rarely now, but still when I need help the messages come – not always at night, but as my diaries will tell, anywhere, any time, especially when I get discouraged or when I need to laugh at myself. At this time however, I found very little to laugh about. All those around me in the church were talking about joy, but there was no joy for me, only a great feeling of responsibility.

. The ministers did not find my message amusing either and I think it was around this time that it was decided that it could be a good idea for them to perform the exorcism on me as obviously I was under the influence of evil spirits. I don't think it did me any harm. It certainly didn't stop me writing or teaching – and everyone was happy enough to let me teach the children for twenty years, both at Sunday School and "Bible in School."

Rest and recuperation

When we left for overseas in the autumn of that year, my first task had been accomplished and I had given the message to the religious leaders in our church. I would never have believed it possible for

God to communicate with humans in a specific way. When I had read in the Bible about the Holy Spirit "coming upon" people like the prophets, I could never have imagined the way in which at first I had felt myself to be in the power of something over which I had no control, but once I had accepted the fact, I was allowed to return to the ordinary world with my own knowledge and reason to guide me. God's timing is perfect, His plans surpass anything mere humans can dream up, and a good servant does exactly what his master tells him to do. If this was an example of the way God planned things, I was going to be quite sure I followed all my instructions to the letter for fear I delayed any of His plans. God has prepared for all eventualities, but since He works through the hearts and minds of people, our running off at tangents and following our own desires as to how we can help, only delays the arrival of the Kingdom of God on earth, that is to me, a beautiful world where all humans live together as part of one family. Perhaps we could have reached that Kingdom before now if the leaders of all religions had stuck to teaching what their prophets had taught. I saw that the crop must be harvested when it is ready or it will spoil. Will we allow it to spoil this time?

The weeds have been allowed to grow until they can be clearly seen. Greed, selfishness, dishonesty, injustice, hatred, cruelty, apathy, laziness - we can see their results so clearly now, *(in religious intolerance, in the business world, in family and other violence like bullying, in our treatment of our environment, and now in our use of communication - the internet)*[12] We must act to control them before they smother the crop, destroy our beautiful world and finally

---

[12] In the 1970s I had been concerned about the direction society was taking. Now in 2015 we have much more to worry about.

ourselves. A good gardener would not allow his crop to be smothered by weeds. He could allow them to grow for a while until they could be clearly identified, but then they would be removed. God is a good gardener and He will try to protect his crop. All of these things had been shown to me as I worked around my own farm. God will produce people who could do the work for him, who could give their lives to working in his garden, but he has also given us free choice. Will enough choose the harder way- good over evil? Will He be given the "first fruits" of the crops of those who will believe the message?"

Another piece from the old folder follows –

"From the heights of the plane on our trip to Europe, just as the light began to touch it I learned, 'It has been a long night, but daylight is near at hand.' As I looked down into the darkness that was below, though the plane was bathed in light, I learned how impossible it is for the people who live in the light to see into the blackness of the lives of the people in darkness. I was also told that I would have to stay down there in the blackness with them and try to explain them and their problems to the people in the light. In London my education continued and in St Paul's cathedral I saw the spiral pillars and climbing vines, and learned that Christianity cannot thrive without the masses, but the masses cannot thrive without the ethical teachings of Jesus Christ."

That is what I wrote many years ago, and later after studying world religions, I came to believe that the ethical teachings of most religions have come from the same source – the force for good in the world, whatever name is given to it by various religions. God is an umbrella over mankind. He is the tree I was shown, that is big enough to shelter all of his people, regardless of race or religion. The piece of writing continued -

"In England, we travelled a lot on the underground, and I learned how vital it is to have clear instructions, and how impossible it is to find your way unless you have a good map or someone to show you the way. You can find your way if you have a goal you can see, but in the dark you cannot see the land-mark that is visible to those in the light. I also learned that even if someone is offering you something very valuable, you may refuse it if you don't speak the same language. And through it all I knew that I was going to have to see that a map was provided, that guidelines were set, that a goal was offered and that I was to be used, because I could speak the same language as the people in the dark and knew how they felt.

I learned that someone opens a gate for you, and you hold a gate open for someone else. I learned that a map is no good if it contains too much information. What is needed for the beginner is simple and clear, uncluttered by the details that may be useful later as you become more experienced. In Italy my attention was constantly focused on the grape vines, and as a farmer, I knew that something was wrong. However there were a lot of grapevines and God takes into account our slowness of uptake. At last I could see what was wrong. The stakes that had been placed in position to support the vines had taken root and were smothering the vines themselves. Instead of a mass of vines covered with fruit, the branches and foliage of the stakes practically hid the vines from view. I knew that the stakes were the Church and its institutions that had grown until the message was practically invisible amongst the trappings and traditions that are a major part of the church today. The message and the vine are still there, but it will not fruit well until the rest is cleared away.

I learned too that one support must not be knocked down until another has been erected in its place, and so the present version of Christianity should not be destroyed until another stronger one is established. Our present period of suffering will be justified when we know that it was necessary for us to see for ourselves how bad a world without God, the force for good, would be. Without experiencing the depths, we would not have the united desire to climb to the heights. We have to want to do God's will because humans themselves must work the miracle. God will put the desire in the hearts of humans and give them the strength, but <u>they</u> will have to act, and in the end they will justify God's pride in His own creation.

I learned that when we are lost in the dark we will head for the nearest glimmer of light. The people who are lost in the dark today, seeing no hope for the world, will be able to find a glimmer of light in a new generation of "children after God's own heart." And I learned that throughout human existence, where the crop has failed in one place, it has thrived in another, and so God's word remains until the soil is right throughout the world, and the crop can thrive without the gardener's attention. (At the time, my understanding was centred around the Christian Church to which I believed I belonged, but it was never my understanding that all people should become "Christians," only that they should recognize one God, the force for good, as an "umbrella over all mankind," and help in the fight against evil). I learned how few material goods people really need, and how too many possessions only complicate life, and so we returned home, with me hoping to clear away some of the clutter in our own lives.

However it takes a great deal of effort to climb out of a rut. Much easier to stay in it unless we are forced to move. When we realize that we are nearing the end of the earth's resources, we will be forced to make an effort, and when we do we will find that with God's help it will be much less harrowing than we imagined."

People will need to be very brave to start another branch of the Christian Church or to start offering an alternative – Christian Beliefs A and Christian Beliefs B. within the church. It could be done. Martin Luther had the courage to question the church of his day. The wandering flock are desperately needed to help in the fight, and they can help without belonging to, or believing in any particular religion. They just need to be on the right side of the ledger when it comes to choosing good over evil.

9

THE FOLLOWING YEARS

O ver the years since the beginning of my journey, the messages have gradually become less frequent. Some of the messages that came were relevant to that particular time, and some referred to the future. Maybe that makes me a prophet of some kind. I did not see myself as anyone special, but only as a person who could be relied on to keep an agreement I had made, and someone who would try to obey instructions. God had told me in the beginning that I was not compelled to do what I was being asked to do. I could choose, but I know that He had known which way I would choose. My only request was that He would protect my family. At that time I was very afraid of evil and how it could work on people's minds to cause harm to others. I had learned that God could bring good out of the harm that evil caused and that He sent people to help us when we were in trouble, but I didn't want my family to suffer. Of course, later I learned that if we did not have to face difficulties and problems we would become very soft, and that every time we find the courage to surmount one obstacle we become stronger to tackle the next one. My family have had plenty of troubles but nothing they have not been able to survive. They will need to be strong when my story is told.

One of the scriptural messages had been that we serve God best if we do what He has asked us to do, and I have always tried to obey my instructions, even if at first, I was deceived about the force that was telling me what to do. It has been impressed on me all along that I must not write or do anything to criticize or condemn other people, but the truth must be told. I learned that God cares as much for the misguided as he does for those who try to do right. He cares for all people and understands what has allowed people to become the way they are, but I must not alter the message to suit the taste of the people who will hear it. He reminded me that the mote in my own eye had been as big as anyone else's and I was always going to have trouble with it. I really wanted to obey, but I was horrified as I gradually realized what I was finally going to have to say. I knew how many of my Christian friends would be upset and how they would see me.

I realized, that to them, it would seem to be a complete betrayal of their faith. I was terrified. When I come to the part of my story that reveals this, the reader will understand why I am so afraid, but also why I cannot leave it unsaid. The slightest feeling of guilt that I have left undone something that I should have done makes me vulnerable to attack from the force of evil, and I cannot face the rest of my life, (however short it may be) knowing that I have left something very important unsaid just because I was frightened of the reactions of some of those who will hear it. I am to present the information as it was given to me. I have been given more light as I have lived up to the light I have already been given. Others can do the same. I had learned that if a person goes to the Bible looking for texts that will confirm their own arguments they will find them, but if people go to the Bible, genuinely looking for the truth, God will draw their attention to it. Those who look for the truth with an open mind will be shown the truth.

Home again and to work

When we returned from our overseas trip, my family and others around me believed hopefully that I had put everything behind me and had returned to normal. I could not tell anyone that I was still receiving messages and that for the rest of my life I would have to work to pass the original message on. The officers of the church had decided at that time that I had been deluded over the message I had tried to give them. I wrote -

"My effort to communicate with the church failed again, quite understandably because if I find it almost impossible to believe what has happened to me, how can I expect anyone else to believe." I knew however, that I had to tell them because the proof would be what happened in the future – whether I managed to fulfill the tasks I had been given, or rather whether God had helped me to succeed in the tasks I had been given. As new vicars took over our church in the following years I was compelled to tell most of them what had happened to me, not all of them, though I had many rational discussions about complex theological matters with some. It is not for me to give names. They will know themselves. I think they mostly saw me as deluded as far as my message to them was concerned, but they still had no objection to my teaching children.

Towards the end of that year, I had been asked to teach "Bible in School," as well as the local Anglican Sunday School. I had agreed to teach the Sunday School as long as it was a community Sunday School like the Methodist church had run in my time as a child, and in my own children's time. "Bible in School" was another matter. This was voluntary time in state schools. I was told that if a teacher could not be found for the Form 1& 2 class (11 to 13 year olds) in the local school, there would be no "Bible in School" for the whole school. I knew most of the people in my community. I knew that for the majority of the children, "Bible in School" would probably be the only organized teaching about God they would receive, and so I could not refuse.

In New Zealand the early European settlers had decided to have a secular education system that was not tied to any particular spiritual beliefs. That was not because they were against Christianity or religion as such. The problem they faced was that there were different Christian denominations, some of which had started up schools of their own and now requested funding from the central government. Most of our settlers at that time had come from different parts of Britain, bringing their denominations with them. Most Anglicans came from England, Roman Catholics from Southern Ireland, Presbyterians from Scotland, and other Protestant churches from Northern Ireland and all over Europe. Who was going to get what funding and whose denomination was going to take what priority in our schools? They all believed they deserved funding because otherwise the government would have to fund extra children in state schools. The decision was made that our education system would not be tied to any denomination. It would be nominally secular. The fact that they were not against Christianity in general was obvious, as a way was soon found to include religious education in the school system. Schools could be officially closed for half an hour, during which time the churches could arrange for teachers to take "Bible in School" classes. A united Church Education Commission would provide voluntary teachers from different denominations for these classes. Most of the Protestant churches took part and provided teachers, but the Roman Catholics and various newer sects remained separate.

In our village school Forms 1 & 2 were taught by the Principal, and the teachers used the "Bible in School" time to hold combined staff meetings. I had believed I had important work to do, but I had not envisaged teaching children, even though one of my insistent messages had been, "Start with the children and be patient." My attention had often been drawn to pregnant women and small children, showing me that my work would be to help and influence them in the future. One message was that God had heard his people calling for help and He was going to try to help them. Another was that though we would start with a tiny spark, we would light a fire that would sweep the world. For me that tiny spark was to accept the task of teaching the local children about God and about the way Jesus had taught us to live - but I had never really enjoyed teaching and I did not accept the idea with enthusiasm. There was a fairly blank period until I accepted the tasks that I had been offered, and then in the middle of February the next year I wrote,

"So now I must write again. I had known that I had to write about what I learned on our trip, but now I know I must get started and put down on paper all that has happened since the account I wrote last autumn. Still shaky after the pounding heart that comes during my nocturnal encounters with the Holy Spirit, but with more confidence now that I know more of the plan. It is true that we have to accept the small tasks before God will trust us with the larger ones. Accepting the task of teaching the Sunday school is now going to lead to other things, that I knew about but was not sure how to get to.

'Children after God's own heart,' is what we must produce. I awoke one night with the knowledge in my mind, and then, 'Carest thou not that we perish? How canst thou lie asleep?' And then the sure and certain knowledge that this was God's answer to our cry. As I had known when I read 'The cross and the switchblade,' and about David Wilkinson's belief that God would lead us into the truth of how to fight the evil that threatened those children, so I knew again that God was giving us the answer. And I knew that I had to write this down, not so that I could get any credit for myself, but so that other people in time to come will know that He answered and kept His promise. He has shown us the way. Now I must work to see that the knowledge reaches the people, and try to inspire them to act on that knowledge."

A while later I wrote,

"Now I know why we have to prove ourselves faithful in the small things, because the larger thing is opening out from this. With the Holy Spirit to guide and direct me, I am to write a book which will be read by many people. It will show them what they must do to help their children rise above the state men are in today. It will give them hope and the desire to work to raise man from the level to which he has fallen.[13] When this book is accepted and the people trust me because they know I want to help them, I am to write another book that will explain God to them. It will make them want to send their

---

[13] Later I was to be shown that my writings would take many forms but the main theme would be the "upright" man.

children to be taught about God, and the Church must provide the teachers washed with the Holy Spirit who will be needed to teach these children. I will be about sixty by the time they read my books, but I will live till I'm over eighty and I will see the beginning of a revival of Christianity. I will go back to Rome some day and talk with important men, and will tell them how Jesus Christ must be held up to draw all men to him. I will tell them about the bread and the wine and the Keys of the Kingdom. In the end they will know that God sent them a prophet."

My timing has been out though. I am now ninety one years old and still trying to get my work accepted. I have managed to get articles published, some in the "N.Z. Principal" that goes to all the schools in New Zealand. Resource books have been written and are on a website with free access for teachers and anyone interested, but I have not as yet made any major break-through. I am trying to get this book on-line now, but am having difficulties because of my lack of computer skills. When we understand how we are up against a force for evil that is working equally hard to see that the message does not get through, we can understand the problems that God has. It is all very well saying that God is all-powerful and then leaving everything to Him, but I have learned that God does not work that way. God speaks to people saying, "Wouldn't it be a good idea to do that?" But evil is constantly putting opposing ideas, "Why bother? It will only give you trouble. Look the other way and pretend you didn't see or hear. Someone else will do it." I have accepted now that I am only sowing seeds. I do not know where they have landed or what the results will be - that is something I do have to leave to God. I have found that in the end God is more powerful than evil, but people need to make the required effort. God does not wave a magic wand

and make everything right. We need to "put on the whole armour of God," and begin the fight against evil for ourselves.

I think I am not making much progress, but when I look back, I can see that I have come a long way from the person I was in the beginning. I would like to see more progress, but I am not dead yet and there is still time. No matter how impatient I am, God's timing is always perfect. The right people may not be in the right places yet, so on with my story. If God wants it written, I will be given time to write it, but I must not waste time. That only gives evil more time to prepare its opposition.

Before I started on my diaries, I wrote messages and lessons down on whatever scraps of paper were available at the time, so now I needed to gather those pieces together in some sort of order. Here is a selection from the early part of 1977 that help to continue my narrative -

"My good friends who don't believe in God will be amazed when they find how God has been able to use them to help me because their hearts are right."

"I know it is an insult to God to offer Him anything less than the best of which we are capable so I applied for a course "Writer's workshop" at Victoria University and was accepted, and now I am learning to type so that I can type my own work privately. From the samples of writing I have already produced, it looks as though I may be writing and interpreting God's standards of righteousness for the man in the street, starting with his children.

I know I have a long way to go before I am fit to cope with what may lie ahead, but God goes on with my training. Strong shoulders and nerves of steel, and a much greater knowledge of God's word than I possess now. Also much less inclination to judge other people and speak without thought[14].

Better put a date on this page of bits and pieces. 9.3.'77"

February 2013 --- Reading these bits over again as I check and recheck what I have written in the past, I had started to add a few thoughts of my own from today about another religion and a thought flashed into my head reminding me of something I was told all those years ago - "Don't get involved in useless theological arguments." I think God was at work again giving me a gentle reminder of my instructions. One good thing about computers is the "delete" key.

More of my notes remind me that my job is to tell what happened to me and offer a way forward, not to try to change those who already have strong beliefs. One of my notes says -

"There has to be a gradual and quiet shift so as not to destroy the church. Older people have a right to be upset if suddenly they are told that what they were taught to believe is not true – but young people and new Christians need to be shown the choice."

In another piece I wrote, "We don't want to lower the standards of the church, but we must cater for the others as well. There must be several lanes of traffic."

And "It is possible to help all of them without trying to convert any of them."

---

[14] I still speak without thought at times and then regret what I have said. No wonder God gave me the job to write and not to be a public speaker.

A verse that was brought to my attention was about finding cattle or sheep wandering, and taking them into the fold. There are plenty of people today who are wandering. They cannot accept everything that Christianity teaches, but they are open to the concept of a spiritual force for good. My work is to offer a viable alternative for them.

Jesus himself said, "In my Father's house are many rooms."[15] Dedicated Christians may believe that everyone will become Christians, but that is not how I see it. I see Jesus' statement as meaning one God for all mankind.

The following piece referred to the way the charismatic movement was leading the church at the time, and was shown to me on a train in Europe, after a guard had ejected an elderly couple from a half empty first class carriage. – "We set our standards too high. We don't care if there are plenty of vacant seats in the first class carriages – nobody with a second-class ticket is going to sit down."

22. 9.77 "You would have thought I would have learnt by now that the voice that speaks urgently in my ear, demanding things is not God. God shows me his messages by things that are true in the world around me, and I believe that the messages that come in the night are from Him. It will be up to others to decide the truth of that. God will show them when they let Him."

I see that year I also wrote,

"No sensible gardener would sow good seeds in ground that was covered by weeds. He would get rid of the weeds first."

---

[15] John Chapter 14 verse 2. ESV

And the grader on the metalled road outside our house at the time, showed me that part of my work would be to "make a straight smooth road for the Lord," Which to me meant teaching about righteousness in a way that would be acceptable in a modern world.

"When we are in a dangerous situation we must have something to which we can cling. The things we must hold to today are the unchanging principles that have worked with Nature and man from the beginning of time.

Greed leads to destruction.

Selfishness leads to blindness

Laziness leads to starvation."

An early page in the big file was a quotation from C.S Lewis, "Mere Christianity." This had been printed in the local Methodist Church bulletin, May 16 1982

"We all want progress, but progress means getting nearer to the place where you want to be – and if you have taken a wrong turning, then to go forward does not get you any nearer.

If you are on the wrong road, progress means doing an about-turn and walking to the right road. In that case the man who turns back soonest is most progressive."

10

TEACHING AND LEARNING

I started teaching Bible in School in March 1977, and during my first lesson at the local school one boy said, "My Dad says this is a load of old rubbish." Another boy said, "We've heard all those Bible stories before." I knew I had to do better, but from my search for interesting teaching material, I felt how inadequate our teaching was at that time for today's world. There was so much material, but so little that seemed to be relevant to these children. We were teaching what we wanted to teach, but they were not learning what they needed to know in a modern world. I thought hard about what I should teach and decided that Jesus had provided the source material and that I should study who, how and what he had taught. I could not go wrong if I followed his example. When he was speaking to ordinary people he taught them with examples from the everyday life around them. He taught them in parables that they could understand. Our society and environment was different, but people are much the same, and also I realized I needed to have a much greater knowledge of the Bible and the teaching of the Christian church. I decided to do a qualification that was being offered by the Church Education Commission at the time, a "Certificate of Religious Knowledge," where I did papers by correspondence, supervised by several different ministers from several different Christian denominations. At this time at the height of the Charismatic movement, one minister had the courage to offer in his course Christian Beliefs A. and Christian Beliefs B., not very radical, but it was a relief to me to see, when I did his paper later that year, that ministers themselves were beginning to ask questions - and so, inadequate as I felt myself to be, I set out on the journey that has already lasted nearly forty years.

After a few weeks teaching I wrote,

"Already God is providing the material for the lessons, step by step. I have learned that if something is not provided, I will not need it. When I looked through my syllabus plan that I had shown to the Minister in charge of the teaching at our school, I realized that there was nothing about the Holy Spirit in the plan up to 12-13 years old, so it is obvious that it is not to be taught at that level. What applies to children would also apply to beginners learning about God. There were more messages. - "Start them on milk" – the milk of human kindness it seemed.

"Make the road straight for God"

"The grass may look dry on top, but there is plenty of green underneath. God has to let us see the symptoms clearly so that we will be able to fight the disease."

"When we get going this time, nothing will stop us.".

I had another of my vivid dreams. This time I was watching church people trying to persuade passers-by to turn to God, but the people just went on walking by. I explained to them that God had said to start with the children, and when they finally decided to do that, we just had to stand back and watch the crowds rush to get what God was offering.

One night I dreamed I woke and saw a white horse standing near me. The next moment I was soaring aloft to dizzying heights and then I awoke breathless and with my heart pounding again. I knew this was only a small sample of what other people would experience when the Holy Spirit is really poured out on earth. I was beginning to realize that I would be writing and interpreting God's standards of righteousness for the ordinary people, starting with the children.

I felt completely inadequate, but by the next month I was writing, "I feel so pleased, astounded and grateful to God for the way things are going. I wish I had David's talent for praise so that I could put into writing how wonderful God is. My own efforts are so futile and muddling, and then God drops in the most marvellous ideas and keeps me supplied bit by bit. I feel such an inadequate teacher, I never seem to do as well as I want to, but the school lessons are obviously going to be the basis for writing where I can be sure of getting said all the things I have been given to say. The "Upright man" is taking shape, and I can see in my mind's eye the cartoons that need to go with it. The Sunday school lessons are easy, but the lessons for school are what really take the effort. By today's standards the children are good, but trying to get through to them leaves me feeling as though I've been through a wringer each week. At least the Sunday school children are there because their parents have a belief in God and the pressure is less."

In June 1977 I wrote, "I have known for weeks that I should write again, but they have kept me so busy I have not been able to find the time. We have been taught to rely on God for everything, but I have found that though God provides the knowledge, the situation and the material, there is always something that I must do myself before we can get any further. So it is with the Kingdom of God. There will be no miraculous event that does not require effort from mankind itself. As I have been shown again and again, no matter how eager we are to help, our help is wasted if we do not do what we are asked to do."

Whatever I did for God though had to be the best I could possibly do. I knew I needed to improve my writing skills and whenever the opportunity arose I attended writers' workshops. I attended a course at Victoria University, though I had to travel overnight by train once a month to Wellington. At that time feminism was just starting to have a major influence on society, and the language in which I wrote would be considered sexist in later years. I still get a bit frustrated with having to consider such things when the meaning seems perfectly clear to me.

The well respected New Zealand historian, Michael King, was one of our lecturers at that course. We had to produce samples of writing for the other students to comment on. Most of the other students were not young, and many had already had work published. For one of my assignments I wrote a story entitled, "What's wrong with being selfish?" It was based on a young person I had known, who had made that remark to me on his wedding day.[16] My article was most unpopular and received severe criticism from the other students, not because of my style of writing, but because of the content, and I realized that often people do not care to have to look at their own actions and their consequences. One older man said to

---

[16] His ex-wife told me recently (2014) that at that time he had been reading Ayn Rand's books.

me, "If they had criticized my work like that, I would not have come back," but of course I did go back, and it was there later that I wrote in an association of words task,

"Spiral pillars
Vine entwined
Sprouting stakes
That hide the vine

Snow-fed rivers
Rising high
Rushing waters
There I lie."

It did not mean anything in particular to me at the time, but several years later when I was reading about the Dead Sea Scrolls, I came across that piece of writing, and had another of those flashes of knowledge as to who lay there and why. No wonder I was worried about what I was eventually going to have to write, and the effect it would have on the way my Christian friends would think of me.

11

EVIL AGAIN AND GOD'S PRINCIPLES

1977 was a year of intense concentration on the work I had been given. Every moment away from farm and office work was spent in preparing lessons, visual aids and song sheets. As if that wasn't enough to concern me, on 14th June I wrote,

"The last time I went to Wellington, 28th May, I arrived home to find that Bill had hepatitis. Poor Bill. If only he knew why he had to be so yellow. Even the doctors find it unusual. They even sent him up to the hospital for special tests. After teaching Sunday School this morning, "they" (the force of evil,) had another temporary victory. They made me be unfair to one of the children just before I left. It was quite strange how I felt myself *used*, to do something that was quite out of character for me. Afterwards I was so worried about everything, that I wasn't completely concentrating on my driving, and when I came to the compulsory stop where I always stop normally, I felt myself *used* to drive slowly around the corner. I could see the black and white shape of a traffic officer's car parked opposite, but as they can do when God removes His protection, they blinded me from registering its significance, until further along the road, the traffic officer pulled up alongside me. Of course then I was so flustered I couldn't find my driver's license, so I had two charges against me, though my license was in my bag all the time. When I got home and found my license in my bag, I found it had expired last year when we were overseas. Licenses had been brought up again and again at work over the last few months, but I had always neglected to check on mine. My license ran out the next day and if I hadn't renewed it then, I would have had to sit all the tests again which would have been worse than any fine I had to pay. If it hadn't been for the traffic ticket I would have been worse off, but for the moment all I could think of was the ticket and the shame of it.

For the next few weeks, evil really went to work I had been told I would be like Job, but now I know something of how they work I can try to be more patient. They were trying to make me give up, but as I know, they would never keep their side of a bargain anyway, so there is no point in making deals with evil. My mother and father are not going to have been sacrificed for nothing. Everything went wrong that could possibly go wrong, but God gives me strength and time. They use kind friends to pile more burdens on me, working on the goodness of their hearts to ring me at inconvenient times and to do things that mean more work for me. One of evil's favourite tricks is to help me make mistakes, and then immediately point out to me what I have done.

God said He would make me strong and now the things that would have sent me into a panic eighteen months ago because they made me feel I was letting God down, I can take in my stride because I have learned that God takes our genuine mistakes and uses them to trump evil's aces. I looked to see how I could use this traffic ticket for God's benefit. "They" kept telling me how terrible it was. People would find out that I had broken the law and so on and so on. I gave a lesson at school about it, producing my ticket and asking the children if they knew what it was. I'm sure I went up in the estimation of the boys, but we used the lesson to show how God can help us in all circumstances. The previous week a boy had tried to elude a traffic officer. He had been stopped and then he stabbed the officer. He was now up on a much worse charge. Because I had admitted my mistake and had been prepared to accept the consequences, I had only been fined, but he had tried to escape and got into worse trouble. It was probably one of the best lessons I had taken with the boys."

I was always concerned about the boys. We had seen how many of the good solid Christian men in our church had been turned off by the charismatic movement. They were not going to wave their arms around and shout, "Praise the Lord!" But the Church needs the good solid "upright" men. My task was to put on the whole armour of God and prove to a new generation of young people that fighting against evil was not going to be an easy option. It was not for the faint-hearted. The meek may eventually inherit the earth, but the strong are going to be needed to see that there is still an earth fit for them to inherit.

Songs like "Fight the good fight," and "Onward Christian soldiers," were needed to inspire them, but the enemy is not other races, religions or people. The enemy is the force of evil and we are all in the battle together. There was another concern for me at that time. The children from Roman Catholic families were being removed from their normal classes, and all ages of Catholic children were being taught together by the local Catholic priest.

My class had been nearly doubled to take in all the year 5s (around 10 years old) as well. The age range had already been too wide and I had felt that I was in danger of losing the older boys of 12-13 years. The inspiration for my lessons had stopped and I knew I had to attend to things in my own environment before I could go on again. When it was time for "Bible in school" classes, the whole school had erupted in a turmoil. The Catholics in my class and all classes left their rooms with their chairs and converged on one room where the Catholic priest had to teach 5-13 year olds. Year 5s left their room with their chairs and came into my room, with the years 6,7 and 8 - and the Jehovah's Witnesses and various others left their classes to occupy themselves in the library. As teachers, we were telling them they were all equally important to God, but by separating them like this we were perpetuating differences. The situation that had now arisen in my classroom showed me what I had to do and the inspiration was provided. I had to write to the Minister's Fraternal, the representatives of all the Churches involved in "Bible in School," tell them what was happening and request their support for the change I proposed

I wrote in my pad, "Perhaps my letter to the Minister's Fraternal is one of the seeds I have to sow. Of course as soon as it was posted 'they' went to work again. I shouldn't have typed it. There were mistakes in my typing. Anything for God should have no mistakes in it. I thought about that when I sent it, and knew what they wanted me to do. No matter how many times I had written it they would always have distracted me into making a mistake. God wants to show us that we must not be afraid of making mistakes. With the best of intentions, mistakes have been made in the past, and we will go on making them. The thing is that God takes those mistakes and uses them as the very things that bring about the victories."

Fortunately in the end everyone co-operated, no-one moved from their own classrooms and at last I had a class of much the same age group of seniors for whom I was able to prepare lessons that were really relevant. – and it has stayed that way.

In my time in a main-stream Christian church, I have not seen that Christianity teaches in so many words that life is a battle between good and evil. Many other religions have done so though. When we were at Sunday School in my youth, my teachers had certainly never frightened us with talk of Satan and hell, but of latter years, the Ten Commandments have also lost the place they used to have. Perhaps, because we are taught that God is all-powerful, and that the name of Jesus Christ has the power to overcome evil, so we have become complacent and are happy to leave it to God. Perhaps it is because that even within the church that is supposed to be teaching God's word we don't want to be made to feel guilty about anything. Did I imagine the power of evil, and should I still have been a psychiatric patient as my father was for the rest of his life?

This is how that previous piece of writing continued,

"If I were to try to tell anyone how 'they' have the power to use animals, the wind, tiny details that cause major problems, no-one would believe me. They do it and they show me they are doing it. To anyone else these things would be accidental or coincidence. I doubt if there are many accidents where evil has not had an input. The "accidental" things that work for good are the work of God. He sends people, and He times events to help us and guide us. The opposition delights in helping us do those things that cause trouble and sorrow. I doubt if Bill's hepatitis was accidental. While he "accidentally" caught hepatitis through an infected person being in the right place at the right time, and through his choice of a particular glass to drink from, my step-father is back in hospital for another operation because of "accidental" internal bleeding after the first operation. No doubt some "accidental" distraction influenced the action of surgeon or nurse."

After I had written that piece I wrote the next,

"Just as well no-one is likely to read this for years, maybe till after I am dead. I wonder what a psychiatrist would think of it."

Since the government has closed most of the psychiatric hospitals now, I suppose I would be returned to the community with a good assortment of drugs as the answer.

I was still writing on pads or on scraps of paper, anything that was available when the messages came. My largest folder contains most of the pieces from those years except for the bits I burned before I learned to distinguish between the forces that were communicating with me, and the material I had given to the Minister after the session of exorcism. God has never asked more of me that I have been able to cope with and I have gone along one step at a time.

I became more confident. By the time I started teaching in 1977 I had God's principles firmly etched on my mind.

Widom, Justice, Truth and Love. For the children it was simple –

Wisdom - We should be sensible.

Justice – We should be fair.

Truth – We should be honest.

Love – We should be kind.

There were two checks and balances to our reasoning-

1. The Golden Rule – Am I treating other people the way I would like them to treat me?
2. A better world – Is this going to make for a better world? At home, at school, at work, in the community, In the environment?

We always used these principles in our reasoning about the situations we discussed. I called them God's principles.

I did not talk to children about the force of evil, but just emphasised that the choices we made should not harm other people or the environment. I said life was like a ball game and we were all players. No-one could sit out. Sometimes we dropped catches, but whenever we did something to help someone it was a point for our side. A lot of the children had been confused about God and Jesus. One thought God was a big eye in the sky watching them all the time. I tried to explain the different roles without confusing them. Jesus was a real person who had lived two thousand years ago and his story is told in the New Testament of the Bible. We can't see God but in a way God is like the wind. We can't see it but we know it is there by the things it does. In the same way God is like electricity or a magnet. If people listen to God good things get done. The word God can be stretched out to spell "good," and God inspires us to do good things.

The principles were simple, and evil's work is easy to understand.

Wisdom - God wants us to use the brains he has given us and consider the long-term consequences of our actions. Evil draws our attention strongly to the immediate rewards of doing things that in the long-term will be detrimental to us and our world, but the voice of God is quieter and less insistent. It is ours to choose.

Justice – God wants us to treat other people fairly. He does not want us to favour any one person or group over another – unless there is just cause - and that would be considered by including the principle of Love. Evil can press for the type of justice that will cause injustice to others. One result of evil's version of justice will be long-term resentment where evil can promote the desire for revenge.

Truth – God insists on honesty and truth, but also that we are honest about our motives in speaking the truth. If we use the truth as an excuse to deliberately hurt other people, we are obeying evil, not God. Decisions we make should be based on as much factual evidence as we can find.

Love – The basis of Jesus' teaching. Few of us can actually love a neighbour who is a constant aggravation to us, but we can care about him as a human being and help him if he is in trouble.

Even if he or she does not do the same, we should treat others the way we would like to be treated ourselves.

These principles were there in the first lessons I took at school in 1977. and one of my notes at the beginning of my folder says,

"We must reach the hearts of the children before the world gets at them and implants its standards."

12

LETTER TO JANE

Looking through the pieces I had written in the early days of my journey, I came across this letter that will explain in simple language what I knew about God at that time. One of my friends was worried that her teenage children were moving away from any belief in God and had asked me to talk to one of them. I decided to write to her and this is the copy of that letter dated 12.10.1977.

Dear Jane,

I hope you don't mind my writing this note to you. It might make it easier for you to understand God. I think all people look for Him, but because they don't understand what they see they decide often that he isn't there. It's rather like saying to someone, "Do you know Mr Jones?" and they'll say "No," but if you say, "Do you know Mr Jones, he's the man who delivers the groceries," they will say, "Of course I know him." God is like that. People know

Him, but they don't know that they do. They have to be introduced.

When your Dad is in England or somewhere away from you, you know he is there and is thinking of you. God is like that, a father you can't see but he is with you in spirit. God is the source of all wisdom, justice, truth and love. His power is the power of love, just like a magnet, seen best when it draws two people together.

If you care about being fair to people you know God. If you believe in being honest you know God. if you care about our beautiful world you know God. If you treat other people the way you would like them to treat you, you know God. God gave us this world to enjoy, voices to sing, rhythm to dance, strong healthy bodies to use to the full, hearts to love, laughter to share and his command to us is to SMILE.

He speaks to us by putting thoughts into our heads, but He gave us free will, and we can listen or not as we choose. Other thoughts come into our heads too, louder than God and we choose who we will listen to. We talk to God as we would to an old friend. Away on your own some time, shut your eyes and think, "Hello God, This is Jane. Are you listening?" And I would be very surprised if you don't hear a small voice say, "Hello Jane. What's your trouble?" and you can tell him all the things you would never tell anyone else.

He makes things happen by using the power of love to send people to help other people. The more people who listen to him the more good things happen in the world. At the moment it seems not too many people in the world are listening to him. Too many are listening to the louder voice of selfishness, greed and envy. This is a good place. I think there are a lot of people here who listen to God even if they don't know they're listening.

You don't have to go to church to know God, but it helps to understand what He is saying if you have a good knowledge of what Jesus said. Then God can flash those things in your mind when you need them. And of course the book of Proverbs in the Old Testament of the Bible contains all the wisdom we need to cope with life today. The modern versions of the Bible are easy to read and very interesting. The people who wrote or translated the Bible were ordinary people and the old stories are not always meant to be taken literally. They are often allegories, stories whose theme repeats again and again. People turn away from God and land in trouble. They turn back to his teachings and things go right for them. Individual sentences and texts from the Bible should not be used just on their own unless they compute with God's principles of fairness to all, and every individual is equally important to God. There is still a lot of truth yet to learn, but the principles are the things we can rely on, and the lessons Jesus himself taught. Love everything good and treat other people as you would like to be treated and your heart will be right with God.

Hope you don't mind my sending you this sermon, such as it is. It may be of some help.

Yours sincerely, Gwen Francis.

Reading that letter over now in 2014, I can see that I could have said a lot more, but I was writing for a specific young person, not for well- educated adults and yet I think it covers the essence of what I wanted her to understand. There is little I would change today, though I would expand on not taking all the old stories literally. They would have been true for the people who wrote them down because that would have been their understanding and interpretation of things that happened to them. Thousands of years of further experiences have widened our knowledge of historical and geographical events, but God's principles do not change.

13

GOD'S TIMING

When we know about God's timing and the way in which He works, we can recognize how in many instances, in our news items about accidents of many kinds, someone with the needed credentials appears quickly on the scene - someone with particular courage, a nurse or doctor - people who are just willing to help. God can use any person in His efforts to help people, atheists, agnostics, anyone of any religion. People who might be outcasts of society, but who are prepared to help each other. Evil on the other hand attempts to make good people look the other way while he influences the weak and misguided to do his work for him.

I wrote this piece about God's timing quite early in the process of my education, though I did not put a date on it.

"One of the things I had always meant to write about as soon as I had time was God's timing.

When I wrote the first brief account of what happened to me in the first months, I said that if I was to write all there was to tell, I would have to write a book.. I feel I should write this because I found it so amazing, but not an essential part of the story at that time

One day I was informed by my voices (or vivid thoughts) that I should go and visit a neighbour who needed help. I was not on really visiting terms with this neighbour, and didn't particularly want to call on her, but obedient as usual, I set out in the car. I had got used to a system of signals by then which showed me I was going "too fast" or "too slow," Another car would come towards me or past me either travelling very fast or very slow, and it would be shown to me as a parable that this applied to what I was doing, and I would accelerate or slow down to order. I arrived at this woman's gate just as she herself was coming out so I didn't actually have to call on her. God had timed my arrival to the precise moment when it would be right for me to stop and talk. She was in need of help and I was able to give her some encouragement and sympathy, without any embarrassment to either of us.

There were many occasions when I experienced these examples of God's timing, so that I could see for myself how He works through people, sending people to help others, arranging what could be thought as accidental meetings - simply because He cares about all people. He does His work silently, and the world cannot see that He is there. Of course evil does the same thing. It also let me see that very clearly, but it works to harm people and make them unhappy. It used to work on me, by bringing the things with unpleasant associations across my path and forcing them to my attention, just as I believe it tempts alcoholics and drug addicts – anyone with a problem – and torments the sad and unhappy."

. My husband often complained that he had had traffic tickets for comparatively harmless misdemeanours, while he saw other drivers doing far more dangerous things on the roads and they didn't seem to get caught. My own belief is that they are not caught at first, because evil has plans for them to carry on and do a great deal more damage - and maybe God did suggest to them that they should slow down or be more careful, but they did not choose to listen to Him. I can see evil suggesting to young people who are fleeing from police –"Go faster! Go faster! They will have to give up the chase," and that is often the last thing they will have heard.

14

MORE WRITING AND ANOTHER MESSAGE

1 977 was a year of acceptance and consolidation. I was now embarked on the work I had been given to do. On the 27th June I wrote. "I was shown recently that I had to tack my writing together before I made the final sewing. I have been sorting all the pieces of writing and 'The Upright Man' is beginning to take shape. There may be more chapters to come, but the bones are there. While checking for material, I read again all that I had written in diary form, and for the second time realized I hadn't written an account of the second message. I had meant to write it down before, when I realized it wasn't there. This time I will not allow myself to be side tracked, and though it is 11p.m., I will not put it off till tomorrow."

The passage continues -

"One night last spring when we had come home from Europe, and when I was being woken regularly at night to get up and write down thoughts that were put into my mind, I was dictated another message. I had written what had been in my head when I awoke and was about to return to bed when there was this strange feeling of being wrapped in power just as I had had before. I had no choice, but was used to write another message, dictated phrase by phrase. Almost the same as the first message, slightly different at the end. I wrote each phrase with no knowledge of what was coming next until I knew it was finished. When I was released from the power that surrounded me, I fell to my knees, completely overwhelmed with awe, and remained there until I had the strength to move. Then I went back to bed, and when I awoke I had to write another sentence. I didn't know whether to write it on the same page because I wasn't certain of its source. I am still worried at times about doing the wrong thing. It's not that I don't realize God can remedy our mistakes, just pride because I don't want to make mistakes. Anyway I wrote it on the same page, and don't doubt that some day someone will find there was a reason for it. I have never mentioned the second message to anyone. It may be many years before it is able to be used. If no-one will believe me about the small things, they certainly won't believe the large ones. When the rest has come true, they may be willing to believe that I am telling the truth. I will be leaving it in the pad with the rest of the writing that I was doing night by night. Other writings may have been inspired, but those two messages were the only ones that were dictated phrase by phrase, without my knowledge of what was to come. The things that I was learning are not going to be popular with the established church. I can see rough seas ahead some day, but God is very good and is preparing my protection. The work I will do for years, the books I will write and the people who will read them will prove that I am obeying God and no-one else. The more that happens and the more that I read the Bible, the more I realize I am doing the right things by accident – God's accidents, which are never accidents at all, only seem so to us."

The messages

I had already been distracted from writing an account of the second message, but I had given the first message to the church and when the vicar asked me for whom the message had been meant, the answer came out of my mouth without any thinking on my part – "For all Christians." I had been told that God had other lights burning under other bushels for other religions and they will know who they are.

I am not sure whether this is the right place to hand the messages on to the public, but one good thing about computers is that you can cut and paste. If later I feel the messages need to go somewhere else I can shift them, but I am putting them on the computer now, at the end of this, so that I can easily find them, and so they won't be overlooked again. I was told that if the church wouldn't listen to me, I was to go to the people and time is running out.

By the time those reading this account get to the messages they will have understood why I am apprehensive about the reaction of Christians and their churches. I am beginning to feel, that to protect me, God will not allow this story to be made public until after I am dead. My poor family will have to cope with the fall-out. I hope they will be strong enough.

* * * *

Now that I have got the messages safely into print, I can go back to my written account from that time. So back to September 1977

12.9.'77

"More lessons and I am reminded of another thing – how evil takes the things God gives us and immediately tries to distort or exaggerate them. I have been reading about the Dead Sea scrolls[17]. My own "teacher of righteousness" is not in human form. I wonder if theirs was. And the "two ways" that have been made so clear lately. If Paul and the Essenes[18] learned from the same source, they didn't need to have had any physical contact at all."

There are missing years after the time Jesus was mentioned as a 12 year old boy, astounding the teachers in the temple by his knowledge of the scriptures. His next appearance in the Bible was as a young man about the age of thirty being baptized in the Jordan by John the Baptist.

Many theories have been put forward as to what he had done during those years, usually that he had gone home to learn to be a carpenter like Joseph. On the other hand the Essenes were known to take boys of that age into their communities to train as scholars and scribes.

---

[17] The Dead Sea Scrolls were found in 1947 and 1952- in pottery jars in caves near Qumran on the Dead Sea. --Mainly books of the Old Testament 1000 years older than previously known copies. Thought to be the library of the Essenes, hidden when their settlement was over-run by the Roman army in 65 CE

[18] The Essenes – A Jewish sect located near the north-west corner of the Dead Sea, renowned for its asceticism, communal lifestyle and strict discipline.

By 2015 we should have learned a lot more from the Dead Sea Scrolls, but I believe there has been difficulty- probably promoted by evil - like all the trouble in the Middle East – in accessing and examining them. If the "Teacher of righteousness" for the Essenes was a human one, and Jesus had been a student with them in those missing years, it is very possible that he may have known more about God's righteousness than the teacher did himself. Did he fall out with them, go out into the world, experience life like any other young man of his age, but come back to John the Baptist to be baptised for forgiveness of the sins he felt he had committed? In the time he spent in the wilderness after that, was he coming to terms with what he believed he was being asked to do? Jesus taught a way of life and the early Christians were called followers of "the way." The possibility that Jesus had spent some of the lost years with the Essenes, could also explain the disappearance of his body before the women came to the tomb. One of my notes tells me that for Jews, it was a capital crime to interfere with a tomb - and that the Essenes kept a different Sabbath day from the other Jews, so they would not have been too afraid to do what they believed they needed to do for him – that is to remove his body from the tomb and dispose of it in their own way.

13.9.77 and I wrote-

"So now I know I must communicate with the church again. Pride makes me find this very difficult, but I know I must be seen to have done what is right in the eyes of the church. Everyone must have a chance. It is not God's will that anyone should be hurt. He shows me He cares just as much for His people as I do for my animals, and there are times when we have to be compelled to do things for our own good. God does compel when it is necessary. We want Him to do things for us and to let us do the comfortable things. He shows me over and over that He provides the materials and the knowledge and the people to help, but we must do the work ourselves. Church people said that God does not compel, but in a way He compels me. Studying, teaching, working for my children. Paul said he was a slave, this force compelling him on. I don't mind giving my body to work, but there are times when I resent having my mind taken over as well, but then I am reminded how much I owe, and it is only my spare time He demands when I am not engaged in my other daily work."

I was still reading the Dead Sea Scrolls and on the 19th I wrote -
"I have been reading the Dead Sea Scrolls 1947-69 by Edmund Wilson.[19]

Goodness gracious me !!! If that is what happens when scholars disagree over the meanings of translations and the interpretations they put on different things, I will have to be very careful. I must get a large book and write everything down in the same book. What they don't take into account is that evil has a cunning habit of hiding things from us, or making our hand slip, or making us write one word when we think we are writing another. That has happened to me many times. Someone could even say that the stroke over the "e" in the line above this (in my notes) means something. All it actually means is that the rings in the folder I am using are getting in the way. The things of God are very simple, but evil confuses us with irrelevant detail. Look at the overall picture. I might also add that evil

---

[19] Unfortunately I did not record any more information about this book then, but later I bought for myself the book "*The dead sea scrolls: A reappraisal*" (1964) by John Allegro in which he deplores the treatment of the Scrolls and suggests they have the potential to build a bridge between the antagonistic faiths of this world. (p 14)

keeps making me forget to get that book to write in, so I have to go
on writing on whatever I have to hand.

Goodness gracious me! Again! If one of my family is going to
have to put this together, for their sake I will have to become more
organized. I must date everything and number pages, even if the
pages I have used up to now are from different pads. (Sometimes
I use z and sometimes I use s in words like organize, just in case
this is questioned. Sometimes my capital Ts are different too.) If I
had known this was going to happen, I would have tried to be more
careful from the start, but I have only come one step at a time so
how was I to know? I still find it difficult to believe. Even the holes
I have punched, where I have written in a pad and filed it later, seem
to have come in strategic places. Not that there is any accident. Evil
is very clever. Pages can be torn out of pads. Leaves can come out of
files – or be taken out, and then evil makes people forget to return
them. There is something to be said for scrolls – an endless scroll
preferably."

20.9.77

"I am determined not to allow myself to be sidetracked this time.
I have kept my mind on "righteousness" ever since I left town. Right
from the start two years ago there was this gentle insistence upon
righteousness. I had to be absolutely honest in all my dealings, things
that had happened right back as far as my school-days – if I felt I had
deceived anyone it had to be put right. I found that if I had anything
on my conscience I was an easy target for evil. Evil played on it and
enlarged it, demanded perfection down to the smallest detail, made
me feel guilty and worried over every little detail. Doing the business
accounts was a constant worry in case I overlooked any little thing.

Now I know that God or the Holy Spirit or whoever it is who insists on righteousness, requires honesty from us, but it is Evil that carries it to such extremes that he tries to worry me over every little detail.[20] As long as I try hard, and the overall result is right, God does not demand perfection in detail. Just that our hearts are right with Him and we genuinely try to do our best. He loves us. If you love someone you do not demand perfection from them."

"21.9.77 Today I had reached the point at which the writer of the Book of Ecclesiastes in the Bible must have arrived when he wrote that particular book. As far as he could see, for all the good he had tried to do, nothing had changed. For all the good life he had tried to lead, for all the wisdom he had tried to acquire and pass on, in the end he was going to die just like any one else and no-one would remember the things he had said and done.

The point of course as God then showed me, is that bare soil will soon be covered with weeds. An empty house will soon be taken over by evil, so while we wait for God we must plant good seeds on the bare soil. We should clean out the house and fill it with good things – the house of our hearts and the house of our world. (**2015** And of course more than two thousand years later people are still reading his words.)

Evil keeps me so busy by sending things and people to make demands on me that I hardly have time to sit down and write. God has shown me that people must always come first, and He will give me time enough. We got a new car yesterday. Evil tried to persuade

---

[20] *"Walking on the water,"* a booklet among my writings, (17 pages unpublished) expands on this.

me it was a gift from God for services rendered. I wouldn't accept this suggestion and this morning I came out to find a flat tyre. A sharp stone had gone right into it. Bill couldn't believe it, but I could. I got my books yesterday, and from now on I will write in them. The longer I go on writing on pieces of paper, the more I, or someone else, will have to sort out. When evil allows me time, I will sort out what I have written already into 1.- personal accounts, and 2.- the information God gives me. I have two books the same, so I will have to put a different cover on one or I'll be tricked again."

In 2015 I need to explain why I would not accept that the new car we had worked for and saved for, was a gift from God for services rendered. The Charismatic movement has almost been forgotten now, but at that time it was very much in the public eye. As many people had forecast, it split the mainstream churches. It also led to the formation of many of the fundamentalist churches, as groups of "born- again" Christians left to start their own churches with their own leaders. These people were genuinely wanting to serve God. I worked with many wonderful people in teaching "Bible in School," even though I didn't agree with everything their leaders were teaching them. One of the things they were being taught was that they could ask for gifts with which to serve God. My argument was that God would choose the gifts he wanted to give. One person considered it was all right to ask for a Cadillac because he needed a car to get around in to do God's work, but my argument was that maybe he needed a car, but asking for a Cadillac sounded a bit greedy.

Today many of these churches are thriving while the mainstream churches languish. Many people tithe their earnings providing their churches with considerable finance with which to do their work and they sometimes erect substantial buildings. Some have radio shows that cater for thousands. Some also provide critics with a lot of ammunition in their criticism of Christianity. Statistics show that they are often the branches of the Christian churches that are increasing their membership. They are filled with goodwill, popular music and everything that appeals to young people and those things should please me. They are filled with good people who want to do good in the world and yet I can see evil at work behind some of their teaching - evil pretending to be God and doing it very well. Some of this teaching could be taking us away from the possibility of bringing religions together to fight against evil. An insistence that every word of the Bible is historically true and a denial of evolution could mean that educated people of the masses of today will reject everything that Christianity has to offer.

15

FAST FORWARD OVER THIRTY YEARS

And so began the diaries, one containing the story of my everyday life and encounters with God and evil since then, and one, containing knowledge or prophecies and advice for the future. After thirty years there were ten pages of messages, but I had filled the other book as a diary by 1997 and decided to continue the diary in the first book, thinking there would be plenty of space. In 2007 I wrote, "There are only about twenty pages of that book left, so the question is, will I need another book or will my work be done in another twenty pages?" By January 2015 I was forty pages into a third book and I am not writing so much there. I was told that I would be a white haired old woman, blind in one eye and lame in one foot. Well, I am certainly blind in one eye and for the last few years I have been lame on and off in one leg - side effects of medication I think. I am not completely white-haired yet though. If the first book covered twenty years and the second covered ten years of my life, I wonder how many years the third book will cover. There's certainly a lot to be said for an endless scroll.

There are a few more pieces in my big file that were written on pad pages around this time, mostly before I bought my books, and I think I should put them in here because they show my thinking at the time, based on what I had already learned. At times I write here as myself, the person I have become over the years. I have learned more. Sometimes my interpretations have changed with further experience, but I try not to change what I wrote in the past. Some pieces have no date on them. Some were written at night or on scraps of paper that were handy. I was still learning so much at the time.

This piece from the big file, 1975-78 gives the essence of what I had learned at that time about the person of Jesus.

"They will say, 'You want to bring down our God,' but that is not so. I need to lift up a man. A man who, being human, not a god, did what he did for love of his fellow men, and because he had absolute knowledge of a power beyond himself. A power he could not deny. He viewed and interpreted that power in the light of the society of the time in which he lived. He did what he believed God wanted him to do. He was prepared to die an extremely unpleasant death for the sake of his fellow human beings. He could have given up criticizing the religious leaders of the day and teaching people how God really wanted them to live, but he chose to carry on. There is less credit for a divine creature that made such a choice, than for an ordinary human being who knew what lay in store for him. God gave him to us as an example of a human as God has planned humans to be. Not exactly perfect perhaps, but made in God's own image – an inspiration to all who follow him."

I was treading a lonely path over these years. I could not confide in my Christian friends. They would have been horrified at what I had to say. The priests to whom I told my story questioned my sanity or thought I was possessed by evil. I could not confide in husband or family. They would also have worried about my sanity. On the nineteenth of September 1977 I wrote -

"I used to wonder why I didn't have a partner when there was the constant idea in the scriptures of going out in twos. God used to remind me that I had Him. Now He has shown me that over a dangerous narrow path, it is necessary to walk alone."

There were always flashes of humour. God often helped me to laugh at myself.

Jan 1978 – No precise date on this because we were staying in an old cabin at the beach (Orua Bay on the Manukau Harbour) and had an extremely uncomfortable bed. God's sense of humour showing here.

"God's laws are not hard and unyielding and uncomfortable. They fit the shape of those who use them. They give support without being rigid. Their basic shape never changes because they are made to fit people - - - and are wide enough to accommodate everybody." The first part was written at night but the final piece was added after three grand-children had bounced into bed in the morning.

And also at that time - "A loving, wise and just God who will allow us to burn our fingers if we persist in playing with fire, but who will see we are not completely consumed by the fire."

Sep 22 1981

Just found this in my desk when I was looking for something else -.

"I still believe that the writing will be important, but I doubt if the timing will be right. The ten years is more likely to be twenty, if not

131

longer. Could be after I'm dead. It doesn't pay to become important. It goes to your head and I'd be no exception. We also have to wait for the children I have taught to grow up. Farming is a long-term thing. I'll put this in my file now because I was told not to throw away anything I had written. It is important for us to see that what is the truth to us at one time may change as we acquire further knowledge, and as circumstances around us change. New wine in new bottles. We must never have closed minds."

Reading through the manuscript again in 2007 I had written here, "But the best wine may have been kept till last. Christianity is being given another chance to get it right. Wisdom, justice, truth and love. These are the principles that God gave me in 1977 and on which I have based the global ethic that applies to all religions and cultures. Christianity has reached a point where choices made now will determine whether any branch of Christianity will survive. Back in 1977, I was shown the oak tree at the top of our farm track that was dividing into two main leaders.[21] I was shown that one branch would go on to become the strong one and the other would become weak. The one that will survive will be the one that is based on God's principles. You will know the truth and the truth will set you free."

On Dec. 9 1976 I had written - 'With the Holy Spirit to guide and direct me, I am to write a book which will be read by many people. It will show them what they must do to help their children rise above the state men are in today. It will give them hope and the desire to work to raise mankind from the level to which it has fallen. When this book is accepted and the people trust me because they know I

---

[21] See p 23

want to help them, I am to write another book which will explain God to them. It will make them want to send their children to be taught about God, and the Church must provide the teachers washed with the Holy Spirit who will be needed to teach these children. I will be about sixty by the time they read my books, but I will live till I'm over eighty and I will see the beginning of a revival of Christianity. I will go back to Rome some day and talk with important men, and will tell them how Jesus Christ must be held up to draw all men to him. I will tell them about the bread and the wine and the Keys of the Kingdom. In the end they will know that God sent them a prophet."

In the year 2007 I commented -

"When I wrote that previous piece on a scrap of fancy paper, back in 1976, I had convinced myself that it would only take about ten years to accomplish my task. One night I think I was dreaming one of those vivid dreams again. The one communicating with me said, "I may be late," and I replied, "I'll wait for you." I am not making any estimation now as to how long I may have to wait.

As for going back to Rome some day – I doubt it will be physically, though my written words may go. The Catholic Church believes it was given the keys of the Kingdom and it will have the power to use them to open the doors to the Kingdom of God on Earth. They must remember Malachi. Do they really believe now that they are teaching the complete truth? Malachi said, "Have we not all one father? Has not one God created us?"

Hard as it may be, accepting the truth about Jesus should be the key that unlocks the doors. I was told not to get involved in useless theological arguments. I am not qualified for that. My task is not to try to convert people who have their own strong beliefs, but to offer an alternative for others and I was certainly out in my first estimation of time.

Jesus himself had believed that the Kingdom of God was near. Probably it could have been if enough people had listened to God rather than to evil. Would more have heard God's words if Jesus had not voluntarily gone to his death? But then if he had not been crucified and if the early Christians had not believed his body had risen from the dead, would Christianity have spread as it did? It is hard to say. Communication was not as easy then as it is today, but even so, it did spread. The crowds had been following Jesus to listen to his teaching while he was alive, not because of anything that happened later. The Gentiles were attracted by the ethical teachings, and probably because the people God had chosen experienced the Baptism of the Holy Spirit - just as the disciples probably did on the Day of Pentecost when the crowds heard them speaking to them in their own languages.

The early Christians who were persecuted for their beliefs, crucified or thrown to the lions would have had to be very sure, and must have had some such experience that convinced them. I often ask myself if I could have been so brave and the answer is, "I don't think so," but perhaps in the company of other believers I might have faced the lions. I might have been ashamed not to. During World Wars people have been prepared to lay down their lives for a cause – though I find it difficult to believe I could have been one of them. I am not naturally brave. Evil may have believed it had disposed of Jesus, but his spirit (God's spirit within him?) lived on and was able to communicate with millions of people since. The story of Easter does not depend on the fact that the body of Jesus had gone, but on the fact that His spirit was still alive and was speaking to them in a different way.

My understanding of what I learned about the Essenes is that Jesus had been one of them and that after he was put in the tomb, they returned, removed his body and buried it in one of their own burial grounds, "Snow-fed rivers rising high, Rushing waters, there I lie."

The one thing that may motivate people to make an effort today is the fear of polluting the planet past the point of no return. The longer we wait to start, the harder the job will be. If Christianity can be discredited, any ethical standards or requirements that are based on religious teaching can also be discredited. Bare soil will soon be covered with weeds and evil's offerings are very attractive. Forty years after I began this journey there is now a greater proportion of the population that is more open to the voice of evil, because the ethical teachings based on religions are being rejected. A genuine fear of polluting the planet may be what is needed for this time.

The Christian story has served its purpose for 2000 years, but the educated masses of today will not accept anything that goes so much against the laws of nature as they know them. At the time of the Charismatic movement I believed that the followers were lifting Jesus up to the point where he was replacing God. I believe the force pretending to be God was encouraging such an emphasis on Jesus because this will keep religions apart. Jesus himself did not say he was God. He called God his father and we are all God's children in that our spirits are part of God's spirit – it is in our spiritual DNA. The Church will need to lift Jesus up as a man so full of the Holy Spirit that he was prepared to suffer a horrible death rather than give up on what he believed God wanted him to do. Once the Christian Church makes this sacrifice, then he really will be able to draw all people of all religions and cultures to him, and the doors to the Kingdom of God on earth will be opened.

I had been told that God had other lamps burning under other bushels and in studying world religions I found a recent example of similar thinking, but no more welcome to Islam than change would be to many in the Christian Church. This group have been in the news recently in 2015, showing the discrimination they suffer in their own country. The Baha'i faith that emerged from Islam just over a hundred years ago is an example of later thinking from the East, emphasising a sole creator, with a single plan for all humanity. It affirms one God for all people and considers Jesus to be one of a line of special Divine Messengers, each of whom has founded a great religion - from Abraham, Krishna, Moses, Zoroastra, Buddha, Jesus, Muhammad, through to their own messengers, The Bab and Baha'u'llah.[22]

I was told we would start a fire that would sweep the world. It only takes a little spark to light a fire when the conditions are right. They seem to be right now. Most countries are part of a global communication system. Most countries with an educated population are rapidly becoming multi-cultural. Most ordinary people have a desire to live peacefully together. It is the influence of evil that will be trying to prevent this. We have been told that in teaching, we must concentrate on the positive, and that is so, but if we ignore the negative

---

[22] The Bab was executed and Baha'u'llah (1817-1892), a Persian nobleman, suffered 40 years of imprisonment and exile. Baha'is have been persecuted in Iran over the last century. Ref. "The Baha'is," published by the Office of Public Information of the Baha'i International Community (1992) Baha'i Publishing Trust of the U.K., Leicestershire, U.K.

things they will not go away. They will only grow stronger. Greed, envy, selfishness, hatred, distrust can keep us apart, but most of all apathy or laziness. Once we make an effort, God will help us, but those Christians (or followers of any religion) who are being taught that they are the chosen ones - who will be saved while the rest of humanity perishes - will need to think again. God has no favourites. Much will be expected from those to whom much has been given. The messages that were dictated so clearly were a warning.

I have mentioned a message that was dictated to me, and then another, but have not written them here yet. I can see why fundamentalist Christians will be eager to reject the warning contained in the messages. I can understand that they are very sincere and they believe what they are taught by their leaders. I can only repeat that God gave us brains and expects us to use them in our search for the truth.

But another message

4.6.2007. Don't drive them into a dead-end with no exit. Allow them a way out with dignity.

16

BACK TO UNIVERSITY

While part of my life over the years had to be unknown to the people around me, the other part was very much involved with other people, and there was much joy and satisfaction to be had. I had family to love, now including more grand-children, work to do on the farm and in the community, and finally back to studies that I really enjoyed. After teaching "Bible in school" for nearly twenty years I had realized that there was a growing movement against such teaching in state schools, even if they were officially closed at the time. There was also a growing movement against Christianity as it was being promoted by the fundamentalist churches that had emerged from the Charismatic movement. I could also see that we were becoming short of teachers, but many of those who were volunteering were from these fundamentalist churches, and some were so full of enthusiasm that they occasionally found it hard to adhere to the teaching code set by the Church Education Commission. By 1995, at the age of seventy one, I had decided to go back to university to study world religions and the similarities in their ethical teachings

Earlier I explained how, when I started at Auckland University in 1941, I joined the Evangelical Union, but left them because I disliked praying aloud in front of others. I also disliked University life because I was alone. No other girls from my rural secondary school had gone on to university and the only boy had taken architecture. I had been glad to leave after two years and go to Teacher's College in Dunedin, to train as a Home Economics teacher, and where girls from all over New Zealand became my friends. In the years since, children and grandchildren have gone to University and it has been a different place for them.

Going back to University in 1995 after a life-time in what I saw as the real world was going to be a challenge, but it wouldn't be so bad this time. Systems had improved. I believed I could do it extramurally i.e. by correspondence with occasional courses on Campus at Massey University in Palmerston North. I enquired whether the papers I had already passed at Auckland could be credited to a B.A. degree from Massey, majoring in Religious Studies. I was pleased to discover that they could, and so in 2001 after five years of extramural study, I was awarded the B.A. degree I had started sixty years before.

This time I enjoyed the work. I enjoyed learning about the religions and philosophies of the world and I had my own agenda. Values education was going to be introduced into schools before too long. I wanted to find the similarities in ethical teaching of world religions and their similarities in values so that eventually I could produce a programme for values education in schools that would be acceptable in a multi-cultural society. I had varying experiences with Professors and lecturers. When we came together for Campus Courses most of our groups were small. Some of the students were young. Few were as old as I was and now I was more confident. I carried on the studies after I had finished the B.A. and gained a Post Graduate Diploma of Education as well as a Graduate Diploma in Subject Studies for teachers (Christian education.)

For the Graduate diploma qualification, I did papers whose lecturers were people from a variety of backgrounds. The papers I took included "Curriculum development in Christian Education," "Issues in Christian thought," "Issues in Christian history," and "Religion and current issues."

I had wanted to do a Master's degree, specializing in values education, but there was no such course, so I settled for the Post Graduate Diploma in Education taking papers that had a high values content, "Ethics in Education," "Current issues in the teaching of Social Studies" "Environmental education," and "Curriculum Design." While doing all these academic papers I realised how so much of the educational research was confirming what I had learned by experience over the years. Now I could question the lecturers when my own experience conflicted with readings we were given. One example was an Ethics paper.

I had signed up for this paper with considerable enthusiasm and was really looking forward to learning more and discussing ethics past and present. I thought that this was one paper in which I should do well. After all, I had spent the last twenty years discussing situation ethics with my classes. I appreciated the academic explanation of the difference between morality and ethics – that every society has its own moral guidelines that set the boundaries of acceptable behaviour, but ethics is the study of our moral beliefs with the aim of improving or extending them in some way.[23]

I was a little disconcerted however, when reading the first set textbook to discover that ethics were seen as an on-going conversation, something that had been going on for centuries,[24] rather than being as I had seen them, based on practical common sense and almost as logical as mathematics. There were many different theories it seemed, and in this paper we were going to study all the theories, but they were still only theories. There was nothing definitive.

Many of the situations that were used in the text books as examples for discussion were situations that were very unlikely to happen in ordinary life, and a great deal of time seemed to be wasted arguing about situations that had no solution that was going to be acceptable to everyone involved. Everyday life however, is full of situations where we have to make decisions. At times we have to compromise. We have to do the best we can. There had to be a simpler answer to everyday problems we are likely to face, and there needed to be consistent guidelines that would be generally acceptable.

Our first assignment in the "Ethics" paper asked the question, "Are Divine Command ethics relevant in today's world?" Divine Command ethics it was explained were ethics spelled out or given by some form of spiritual power. Under this theory actions are right because a God of some kind commands them. At this time I was thinking no further than the Divine Command ethics that I knew personally. I thought of the Ten Commandments that had been the ethics of my childhood, and I thought of the "New Commandment" of

---

[23] Hinman L. (1998) 2nd edition. *A pluralistic approach to moral theory.* USA: Harcourt Brace and Co. p 5.

[24] Hinman p 3-5

Christianity - the golden rule that we should treat other people the way we would like to be treated ourselves. Were the ten commandments still relevant? It seemed to me that if we left out the first two about worshipping a specific God, the rest were just as relevant as ever. Respect your parents. Rest one day a week. Do not steal. Do not tell lies. Do not commit murder. Do not covet something that belongs to someone else. Do not commit adultery. Had all of these "do nots" now become acceptable because "everybody does it'" or were they still wrong in principle because they harmed other people? And what about "You shall not worship idols?" Were we making idols of possessions and money? I thought of sport as it had been when we were younger, and when the honour of representing our particular area was our greatest ambition, and sport as it has become today with the millions of dollars attached. I thought of big cars, the right labels on clothes and the latest models of all kinds of technology. There appeared to be a reasonable argument that we were coming to worship money and what it can obtain for us.

Then of course there was the Golden Rule. It appears in some form in all the main religions, and even humanists accept it as a reasonable measure of behaviour towards other people. I thought I could develop some good arguments along those lines. I felt that I could produce a very good assignment. B + at least. Maybe A- ?

My assignment was returned with a D. Failed! I had missed the point of the argument. Divine Command ethics were out because a Divine being could command horrible or cruel behaviour of any kind and it would be accepted and obeyed just because the Divine being had commanded it. It was no use my arguing that the God I had learned about in my childhood was a God of love and would not command such things. There was plenty of evidence that even Christianity had been responsible for much cruelty in the past.

The story was brought up of Abraham who was preparing to sacrifice his only child Isaac, because he believed God had commanded him to do so. This is a story from the Old Testament of the Bible that is usually interpreted within the church as God testing Abraham's faith. After all God had told Abraham that his descendants would be as numerous as the stars in the sky.[25] Abraham and his wife were very old and if he had sacrificed Isaac there would have been no descendants, but Abraham did as he believed God had asked him to, and was about to kill his young son on the altar he had built when he heard an angel saying to him, "Stop! You have proved yourself," Abraham turned round and saw a ram caught in a bush and was told he should offer the ram as a burnt offering in place` of his son. I find it difficult to believe that a loving God would have put Abraham through that torment, but I can very well believe that evil had been pretending to be God in an effort to prevent Abraham having any descendants. God's timing is perfect though and the ram arrived in the right place at the right time to provide a substitute sacrifice.

The Bible –

This seems to be the place to include some information about the Bible itself. This is needed because both university lecturers and writers like Richard Dawkins[26] base many of their criticisms on the literal meaning of the words used and claims of their historical

---

[25] Genesis Ch 15 verse 5
[26] The God Delusion

accuracy. The Christian Bible has two parts - the Old Testament and the New Testament. Jews, Moslems and Christians are all said to be "People of the Book," because their histories go back to Abraham in the Old Testament. This Book is a collection of books (writings) that provide the story of the three religions up to the birth of Jesus Christ. The New Testament is the Christian story from then on, and our dates change from B.C. (Before Christ. Now B.C.E - Before Common Era) to A.D. (Anno Domini i.e. The year of our Lord, now changing to C.E. - Common Era.) All mainstream religions have their Holy pieces of literature. Islam has the Koran where the teachings began with Muhammad in the 7th Century A.D. There is enough factual evidence today about the Bible and how it was written, that it is difficult to cling to the argument that everything written there is literally and historically true, but evil encourages this claim because it allows valid argument against the Bible as a whole.

We need to see these stories within the times in which they were written. The writers could only interpret events in the light of the knowledge available to them at the time. They were people of their day with the limited understanding of God that they had then. Take the story of Noah for instance. It has been common to picture Noah as taking two of every species of living creature in the world into the ark. Common sense suggests that the story of a great flood is based on an actual event, because the story appears in the traditions of other groups as well e.g. The epic of Gilgamesh, a good man who lived in a city on the banks of the Euphrates river, and was also warned to build a boat to save his family and animals. It would have been sensible for a person who believed what God was warning him, to take with them, pairs of the domestic creatures they were going to need when the waters went down. It seems that there really had been a huge flood that covered the world as they knew it at that time. What would have happened if the waters of the Atlantic ocean had suddenly broken through into the Mediterranean Sea at Gibraltar?

We know that myths and traditions are often based on actual events that have happened in the distant past. We can not take every word in the Bible literally and as the absolute historical truth for all time. Christianity broadened our understanding and brought a different picture of God. Maybe in Old Testament times more primitive people needed to be frightened into good behaviour by an "eye for an eye" system of justice. Christian teachers of today do all Christianity a disservice when they claim that every word of the Bible is literally true. Anyone who has the time and inclination to go through the Bible verse by verse can find discrepancies of various kinds. Thirty or more years ago I was given a paper that was circulating amongst university circles pointing them out.[27] As the author said in some of his final words.

"I believe that scientists have to reclaim the Bible. We should be urging that it be taught in the schools, not by those anxious to sustain a narrow faith, but by people who understand it and respect it. It is one of the great achievements and basic works of the whole of western culture. If we desert it and abandon it to fanatics, we have only ourselves to blame when it rises to haunt us, transformed beyond recognition. (p 37)

Back to ethics then. In my ethics assignment, I had been looking at the question I had been given from the point of view of a modern-day

---

[27] (1983) McGlone, M. Scientific creationism: The Bible says No. See notes at the end of this book

average Christian, but as the lecturers reminded me, the God of the Christians, Jews and Islam was not the only god - if there was a god at all. Horrible things had been done in the past. Human sacrifices and blood-shed - all because the gods required it. I had to accept that, and also that it was still going on today – and though I believed that those committing such horrors were obeying evil and not the God I know, the evidence was clear to others. As for the Golden Rule – "there is too much scope there for sado-masochism," was the note written on my assignment. After I had looked up the dictionary to make sure I understood what that meant, I felt that it was very unlikely that many people would want to inflict pain on other people simply because they enjoyed suffering themselves. – but that is what ethics is all about -. ongoing argument - and Christians were supplying ammunition themselves.

In the end after much discussion backwards and forwards with the lecturer, I was finally given a C for the assignment and I had learned a very valuable lesson. If there was ever going to be an ethical formula that was generally acceptable in a multi-cultural society it would not be one that relied on any religion as a basis for acceptance – because a modern educated secular world would not accept it.

During the course a question was asked that had often come up in my classes at school with regards to protecting a friend. They had been learning about virtues. Honesty is a virtue. If it is accepted that we should be honest, would it be ethical to lie to save someone from the consequences of their actions? In real situations, the virtue of loyalty can conflict with the virtue of honesty.. It was very important to the children. "Should we snitch on our mates?" Aristotle offered an answer here when he offered the middle way. Speak the truth whenever it is reasonably required, always look for the truth, but a lot depends on your motive in telling the truth and when and to whom it is told. At school when the question was discussed we usually ended up by deciding that if a whole class was going to be punished because of the action of one person, that person should own up themselves. What sort of a friend would deliberately let others take the blame for his actions? If that action might endanger or harm other people then the information should be passed on to some other responsible person who could do something about it. Consequences as well as loyalty had to be taken into consideration. Motives as well.

As a parable, this is a problem that is going to have to be faced by those who do not really believe that everything they are required to teach is the truth. For the sake of future generations, should they be loyal to the Institution of the church – or the dogma of the church - or will they follow God's requirement for truth?

"No offence intended but" -- It was pointed out to me recently that the user of this introductory phrase usually went on to make a point that may have been true, but was also hurtful to the recipient. Lessons on virtues and honesty in school had given the speakers the excuse to upset others, and an examination of the motives of the speakers would have shown they were less than virtuous. Even virtues need to conform to ethical principles. If it is really necessary to expose an unpleasant truth for reasons of justice, or because of the possible consequences of not telling the truth, at least it can be told kindly. If parties continue to differ, they can choose to go their separate ways and part in friendship without acrimony.

Possibly the Christian church is going to come to this stage. My understanding is that there will be two branches and one will outgrow the other. My instructions for the churches is that they are not to try to destroy each other. One must not be knocked down before the other is in place. Then they will see. It will be God's choice which branch the masses will accept and which branch will survive.

In the ethics paper we studied a range of different ethical theories from Utilitarianism to Kant, to race, Aristotle, and gender without coming to any conclusion as to whether one theory was more useful or practical than another. I could see that no one ethical theory was going to give me what was needed - a simple ethical formula that everyone from small children up could understand, and that could be acceptable in a multi-cultural society.

One theory was new and alien to me. To someone like myself, brought up on precepts about "helping your neighbour" and "going the extra mile," the theory of "Ethical egoism," seemed to promote selfishness and individualism, but I could see the point of the argument even if I couldn't accept the theory. We are all a bit selfish. The promoters of this theory claimed that someone like Mother Theresa appeared to be acting purely for the sake of other people, but she did what she did out of self-interest. It made her feel good.[28] There is certainly truth there, but not the whole truth - and the individual does matter – but not to the exclusion of others. One of the theorists arguing for ethical egoism had been very influenced by the religious moralising he had received in his youth – that everyone else was important, but he was not.[29] That is going to the other extreme.

I learned that much contemporary work about ethical egoism had been inspired by Libertarianism, and by the novels of Ayn Rand, such as "Atlas Shrugged" and "The Fountainhead." At first glance, Ethical

---

[28] Hinman, p 122
[29] Hinman p140

egoism, libertarianism and an emphasis on freedom do sound quite reasonable - until you ask a question that Kant would have asked, the categorical imperative, "If an action is all right for me, it must be all right for everyone else, so what would happen if everyone did that?" Then it seemed to me that if everyone put their own interests first we would live by the law of the jungle – survival of the fittest, and it seemed that Kant had an important point, and a question that needed to be asked in any ethical assessment of an action. For instance, "Why is it important not to tell lies?" If we ask the question "What would happen if everyone felt free to lie to each other?" we can see what sort of world we would live in if there was no-one we could trust. We can see why being honest and looking for the truth is important as a general principle in community life.

Just as I had argued from my own background that a God of Love would not command his followers to do anything cruel or harmful, most of us have ethical capital from past teaching, Reading Ayn Rand's books, the average reader presumes that Ayn Rand's hero was an ethical man at heart and he would not deliberately harm others by his actions, but we are presuming a background of ethical capital that is slipping away, is not being replaced – and is not common to all young people today – even in westernised societies.

White-collar crime today shows that a good education and a high IQ does not necessarily result in high ethical standards. In a newer world where so much emphasis has been placed on individualism, researchers are now finding that the excessive individualism that has dominated our culture over recent years, separates individuals from their context and deprives them of a larger sense of connection and meaning.[30]

Once again it is excess that is the problem. Every individual is important to the God I know. It seems that what we really need are individuals who see themselves as part of their community and who focus their talents on the welfare of their community as a whole, rather than making a priority of their own religion or their own advancement. We should be very worried about modern technology that separates people from the real world - and its effect on the young, who may find it difficult to separate "virtual" reality from the real world of people who have feelings and can be hurt or harmed. New research is even showing that people who spend the most time communicating through modern technology can also be the most depressed. If happiness is about contentment and is maximized when a person also feels part of a community, individuals would probably be happier spending more time with real people in the real world. An individual who has walked over others on the path to success can end up being very lonely.

If we ask what would happen if everyone considered other people's interests before or as much as their own, the answer would be that while I was putting your interests first, you would be putting mine first and everyone would end up happier. Isn't that what the Golden Rule is really all about?

---

[30] Berman, S. (1997). *Children's social consciousness and the development of social responsibility*. P66

17

THE POWER OF LOVE AS A LAW OF NATURE

As time went on, though I still just followed, step by step, what I believed were my instructions, I came to learn more and more about the ways of God. At the end of 1997 I wrote the following - (I have brought a very small amount of thinking about modern technology up to date with the advances that have been made over the years since then. Cell-phones and I-pads had not taken over our lives at that time.)

4.12.97

"Recently I was driving home on our reasonably quiet country road, letting my thoughts follow their own path. God often uses this to lead them to things He wants me to see, but I don't consciously set out for this as a person might do in meditating.

I was wondering how God has so much power that He could know about and speak to people all over the world at the same time. I know that love has actual power like a magnet. Probably not so noticeable today when sexual attraction seems more generally recognized as love, but if two people are attracted to each other, like each other, enjoy being with each other, but do not touch each other sexually, the power can grow much more intense.

Thinking about what I had learned in the beginning about the answer being the power of love, the infinite love of God for mankind, I was thinking that it had to be a force that operated all over the world at the same time – and always the same – like the law of gravity – and that flash of knowledge that God gives me when He shows me something, showed me then.

Yes!!! A force – a natural law - like the law of gravity. The force of love acts for good everywhere, in all situations. It is a law of nature, inexplicable though it may be to us at this time, but it will be a challenge for scientists to try and discover it.[31] I guess it would need two scientists in love with each other, caring about each other, but resisting the attraction till they found how to measure it. Impossible? Maybe it is impossible for humans to measure, but it is not impossible to conceive once we put our minds to it. Look at all the modern information technology that was never dreamed of in the past- the size of the first computers and the small gadgets that are inseparable appendages to most people in our modern world.

Harder to accept is that there is also a force for evil, a malevolent force that hates humanity and operates in the same way. I felt its malevolence once when God allowed me to feel it, just to show me what it would be like if evil took over the world. It was horrifying and

---

[31] Richard Dawkins is on the right track. See later in chapter on *The God Delusion*.

I never want to feel it again. I don't know how it works. Perhaps power is generated when people do good things, and power is generated for evil when people do things to harm each other or the earth. If this is so, then what is needed is more people doing good than doing harmful things, and each person can do his or her share, just in their own little circle, to turn the tide."

On 7th June 2007 I wrote -

"I said I never wanted to feel the malevolence of that force again, but God allowed me to feel just a flash of it again just recently in another vivid dream. I had known that the first part of my work was nearly done, not perfect and it could still be polished up a bit, but it was there in print. I had known that I should start on the second part, but I was tired. I was putting off the effort, and I was spending my evenings in my armchair, comfortably knitting and watching the TV. It just seemed too difficult to get started again spending my evenings upstairs at my computer and all my spare time as well. I felt the malevolent power in a vivid dream, and the next day I was also allowed to experience its force when I was driving my car into the town. Just before I left, my husband asked me to do something for him in town that he could have done for himself when he was there the day before - and note this is how evil works. I already had quite a list of things to do and one more was the last straw. I usually talk myself out of my mutterings about people adding to someone else's burdens, but this time I just didn't seem to be able to shake it off, and I went out with my mind full of my grievances, instead of being completely concentrated on the other traffic on the road. At a round-about, I was quite confident that I had carefully looked to my right to give way to traffic coming from that side, and absolutely couldn't believe it when I finally saw a car right in front of me. I clipped the back corner of his car, but practically demolished the front few inches of mine. Both headlights, bumper, bonnet etc. I don't think the driver of the other car could believe that I had been so stupid, but I knew immediately what had happened. I had been allowed to experience that evil force again in a minor way, and I had been so wrapped up in my own grievances that I had been completely blinded to what was going on around me. God is gracious and no-one was hurt. The air-bag hadn't gone off. The other driver wasn't happy, but I admitted immediately that it had been my fault. A nice young man from a house nearby rang our panel-beater and offered me a cup of tea while I was waiting, and our panel-beater arrived, arranged for my car to be towed and took me home. Another metre forward, or if I had been going a bit faster, and the other car would have hit me right in the driver's door.

I had needed to be jolted out of my complacency in thinking there was plenty of time for me to get on with my work. God does not punish us, but He can remove His protection and allow us to experience what life would be like without it. So now I am writing again and enjoying it knowing that I am on the right track again.

God's timing is always perfect, even if we slow it down by our reluctance to make the effort that is required."

I said there that God's timing is perfect and I don't want to be misunderstood. It is not that God chooses when and where things will happen and so humans act accordingly. What I mean is that God gave us free will. He knows how we will act or how we will put off acting and keeps the bases covered.

18

VALUES EDUCATION

V alues education took over the next part of my life. In 2005, the year I finished my Post Graduate Diploma of Education, the Government published a report it had commissioned into the teaching of values in schools. The word "moral" had become unpopular because it was too much associated with religion. Now the emphasis was on values education, not "moral" education. Amongst other things, the report had stated that there would need to be strong resource and professional development support for schools and teachers.

Right from the beginning I had known that I was going to have to put the lessons that God had given me for the children into a form that would be acceptable in a secular society. There would be no reference to religion as the authority as there had been in Bible in School. These lessons would be based purely on reason, and as one of my main projects for my Post-Graduate Diploma of Education I had designed a programme for values education in New Zealand schools. I contacted the Ministry of Education to ask if they would be interested in looking at it. The reply was "No. The Ministry is not responsible for resource material. Schools choose their own. Go to an Educational publisher." And so began another journey over the next two years that took me full circle from the Ministry of Education to educational publishers to Ministers of education, to members of parliament who were on the Select Committee for education and science, and finally back to the Ministry of Education without finding anyone who was responsible for seeing that resource material was provided. There was always someone else I could be passed on to. Finally a new Minister of Education arranged for me to have a free advertisement once a term in a ministry publication, and for me to have an interview at a University with the academic who had been responsible for producing the report. My books began to become known a bit more widely.

By 2007 a new Curriculum had been finalized, but there was to be no actual values education. Half a page covered the issue. There was a short list of generally accepted values that were to be encouraged, modelled and explored. Excellence, innovation, diversity, equity, community and participation for the common good, ecological sustainability and integrity were the stated values, and children were to respect themselves, respect others and respect human rights. These values were to be evident in the schools' philosophy and relationships, and students were to develop their ability to make ethical decisions and act on them. The general outline sounds fine and schools are doing their best to promote these values, but it is not possible to make ethical decisions on the basis of generally accepted values, especially in a multi-ethnic or multi-cultural society. According to official figures in 2015 there are now 200 ethnic groups in our largest city. Diversity is a stated value, but not all values of all groups are ethical values. Some traditional cultural ceremonies involve cruelty to other people or animals. Helping family first can be seen as a value in some societies, but it can be seen as nepotism where others are concerned. Groups can still claim special treatment because of race or religion, but are the cultural values of one group more important than those of another.? Equity through social justice may not mean the same thing to everyone. Schools and teachers however have to deal with real situations and make decisions.

Because there was no specific place for values in the curriculum, educational publishers were not interested in publishing my material, so I self-published two of my books, but publishing small numbers makes them very expensive. Even photo-copying is expensive for schools that claim they are always under-funded.

By this time I had set up my own web-site where anyone would have free access to the basics of my lessons. The ethical principles that could be used in making ethical decisions in a multi-ethnic society were there.. A number of books have been sold all over the country. I have donated books to the libraries of our main universities and copies are with the national library. Finally I managed, with the help of a neighbour - who I will always believe had been sent to help me - to put them free on-line because that is the most practical way now of getting them to the people. At least I have spread enough of them around to sow seeds, and so that in the future the information will not be lost.

It was suggested to me by one publisher that the book, "Forty lessons on Citizenship" could be rewritten as a book for the general public, though it would take a lot of work and I would be the only one who could do it. Over the last two years of my husband's illness

I worked on it as a semi-autobiography, writing for later generations. I named it "'Upright' in the 21st Century." By this time the publisher decided with regret that under the present publishing conditions it would be too risky to publish it, but I am not sorry that I put the work into it. It will be there for my descendants and I have sent copies to the National Library as required. Someone may find it useful some day as a social commentary.

Some people have told me my work is too simplistic, but things from God are always simple. If we teach children from the youngest age to think about the consequences of their actions – to be fair- to be honest and to be kind, the same principles will be relevant all throughout their lives. Even in the most complicated situations in our adult lives, the same principles are guidelines for our reasoning, and something solid to hold on to. As I learned on our first visit to London, a map can be difficult to read if it has too much information on it. I think I have done as much as I can to offer the teaching in a way that will be acceptable to the educated secular masses of a modern world, and I have no idea who accesses my web-site, or where seeds have fallen. As I said at the beginning, whenever people have done something to help someone else, they have been listening to and helping God.

It is unfortunate for Christianity that during the enlightenment of the eighteen hundreds so many of the best brains rejected the church because of some of its teaching. I think that during the Charismatic movement of last century God was offering a trial run to see what the mainline churches would do with the power that could be available, but again the way it was sometimes used influenced a number of our "upright" men to walk away from the institution of the Church.. At times together with family they were always big days. Plenty of food and drink,well that was another Christmas day gone. They come as quick as they go, then it's boxing another day of food and drinking. We had some great times at mum and dad's house Well I'm on holidays for 2 weeks,so planing on going out fishing in our boat with mum and dad. We used to pump yabbies it was hard work, or we would buy blood worms. They were 5 dollars a dozen,we would always catch a good feed of whiting,we used to buy blood worms off some frieThey were my aborigines friends that live on a island they were great friends. We enjoyed our fishing we have great memories. While I was fishing I was off the drugs and beer. We would give some fish away to friends and family, there was always to much for us. We just enjoyed the time together as a family, and the whiting were great fun to catch. Mum would give dad and me a hand to clean them,that was the worst part about catching them. Mum and dad bought this toboggan, for me to get towed behind the boat. There was one day we were over other side of the bay, near beach,and I fell off into a big school of big brown manaors jelly fish. And they stung me all over my body,and I was yelling and screaming. I could hear mum saying he's been taken by a shark. They quickly came over and pulled me into boat,your alright mum said no I've been stung by those jelly fish. I never rode it again. There was hundreds of them in the water, they were every where. Went dad started the boat up and took off, you could feel them getting hit by prop. There was no way of missing them, that day we had a bbq nothing like fresh fish cooked on the bbq. Dad and I would have a couple beers as they cooked,and mum would prepare the salad. The following weekend was dads 70th birthday on saturday night. Mum and I had arranged a 11 gallon keg as a surprise for dad. Before dad left to go and play bowls,at club. gave me a job to do, was make sure I put his bottles of home brew in his beer fridge in garage. And told me make sure your mum doesn't put any food in it,ok dad you can trust me. We had a guy from the club come around, and set keg up as it needed to be settled down. Then mum and I continued get things ready.Dad arrived home from bowls,he said did I take care of his beer. Yes dad we had half a dozen bottles of home brew in fridge. I said to him come out near the pool,I will buy you a beer. Dad was so surprised what a great idea he said. Poured him a beer it was perfect, so we had a beer. Then he went and got changed. Ready for a big night of family and friends,I was at the keg most of the night. Pouring drinks It started pouring not so good,and you always get the experts I'll fix it. I said leave it alone the cellar man said not to play with it, just give it a rest for a while. And it started pouring good again,people thought it was a great idea. And works out cheaper than cartoons. Was time to cut the cake and blow out candles, I'd made a plague from timber had engraved happy 70tn birthday day. It was painted with two pack paint and gold letters. Dad loved it, we had it hung up in garage, the night was coming to a end. Everyone had enjoyed them selfs,the next morning there was about 3 gallons left in it. The neighbour across the road, Charlie and betty had invited us over. So we took keg over to finish off They were good neighbors to mum and dad. I said my good byes as I was back to work on monday. Arrived home had a bbq for tea, couple of beers and some cones. I had been hanging out for some cones,since friday you get used to having it every day. Well it's monday start of a new week,need to start day off with some cones. And every day I would say to myself, when will I ever get over this pain. As I've said before my life could of been so much different. Getting stoned every day,and drinking most days. And getting drunk of a weekend, it's only temporary so you start all over again. Be days were I would run out of heads grass hash,and have no money to pay day. Because I had a good credit rating,I could score any time. Had about 3 dealers if one didn't have anything, I could always get it off someone else. When ever I got some good heads, I would save the seeds and plant them. The plants were never as good as what I would buy, but it was free smoking. One of the dealers ask me if I wanted to sell for him,I thought this was great. He had putty black hash at the time and he gave me some blocks to sell. I never sold them I'd keep them so I had heaps to smoke. It was not a good move, but I had a problem and it just started to get worse. As the days weeks months years went on,I kept saying to myself I need help. I didn't want to tell mum and dad. but my problem continued everything had just become a habit. I felt so good when I was out of it,I was so happy but everyday the pain just followed me. A couple of years has past since my dads 70th birthday, and things are still the same with me. Still working smoking drugs and drinking ever day. A couple of weeks was my mum's 70th birthday,and we are going to port macquaire for the weekend. My aunty and one of my cousins lived there,we left early The hardest thing for me is when I'm with mum and dad,I'm unable to have cones. When your away so I look forward to it when I get home, We arrived and jeff took mum down to the town ship, and bought her a soft serve ice cream. It was pouring with rain jeff said are you ready to get your feet wet. said we have booked you a ride on a para flight. Were you get towed behind the boat, mum's replie was not on your sweet life. He had mum going so we went back to my cousins, had a few drinks the ladies had scotch and the men had beer and we had some picks. There always good had to go past chicken in the biskit cheese dip. We were going to one of the clubs for mum's birthday dinner, we always enjoyed going up to port. As we had my cousin and auntys place's to stay,plus my other cousins would be there, Was great catching up with them,as we don't get to see each other now.As we have all gone our different ways. So it was always special when we met,and have a laugh.The only thing wrong I think is the time goes so fast. It was time to get ready go out, we arrived at the club to celebrate mums 70th. The food was lovely a good selection, beer was good. It was great to catch up with the family, we all had a good time. I went to bed when we got back to cousins house. It was a lounge pulls out to a bed,every time I rolled over I could feel a steel bar. So I didn't get much sleep. We left early sunday morning called in to get fuel,and went to McDonald's for breakfast.We had a good trip home,I was looking forward to my bed. Couple of beers and some cones,now I was feeling better. Back to work on monday,next party was my 40th which we are having at mum and dads. Looking forward to that the boss came and saw me,will you be ok to go to drive over night. So I had to work a full day load truck in the afternoon. Go home have a shower get changed and get on the road,for 7 hour trip,was not looking forward to it.I was passed sydney on the hume high way,had the cb radio on listening to the truckies. It's a busy road I was having trouble staying awake. So I pulled off to the side of the road, got out of truck had a walk around. I was feeling better so I resumed driving, just went through goulburn. And the police pulled me over for breath test that was all good,so I continued I was approaching the federal high way. The road is wide there hume 2 lanes and federal high way 2 lanes. This is were I fell asleep behind the wheel for maybe a second. Heard a noise and woke up that was not good. So I found a pull in bay and thought have a couple hours sleep,no bed in truck had to lay across seat. Not real comfortable managed a few hours sleep. And got back on road to be at my drop off point by 7am,arrived had a smoke coffee bit of a rest. Then we unloaded truck got paper work signed,then I was off back home. Would of been nice to go book into motel for the day,but I had to be back at work that day. So you work the hours out from monday 8hr day then drive to canberra 7.5 hrs driving. Pulled over for 3hrs then trip home 8hrs with 3 hours sleep for 2 days not good. Arrived back at work told boss that was total madness what I just done,lucky to be alive. So I explained to him his answer was I'll get someone else. And to do what I done yes was his replie,I said to him it was only that I have had a history of truck driving that I'm back here save. And you going to put someone in that has done little driving. I said the only way to do it save is to book into a motel,and come back the next day so thats what he done,so I continued doing all the drving. I loved driving out in the open air your own boss.Well it's been a busy week, so first thing go to club get wages cartoon of beer bag of ice. Go home put beer ice in esky,now for shower couple beers some cones. Then walk to the pub for a great night, this was my usual thing each weekend. Just get totally wasted as each day that goes by,I still suffer with the pain of my 21st. Then after night at pub and club, I would stagger home have some cones then go to bed. Each morning would wake up with a shocking hang over,so I would have a few beers and cones for breakfast. Then have something to eat couple more cones then back down to the pub,for a day of drinking playing pool. I was begining to think I need a change,but I would just keep thinking. Bad habits are hard to shake so I just continue doing the same old thing. Work 5 days have 4 beers each afternoon up to thursday and cones morning at work night. Then get drunk friday and saturday nights what a life.Then sundays I would dry out sobber up ready for work again.Some friday nights I would hang out at the club, the guys that lived there was were good friends. And we would have oysters 20 litre bucket, as they worked on oyster leases. And we would have port beer spirits, we had great times it was close for me to walk home. We had big partys there would go for two days. We had old lounge chairs car seats had a big double shed down the back,big bbq which was used alot. Was a timber one when we finished cooking,take plate off and put more timber on. To keep warm in winter I remember one night.Pete said you don't need to walk around the street way,he took a fence post out said there you go. Now you have a short cut home,as I lived in caravan park at back,so it was handy for me. Well another weeks work a head, so it all starts again I'd have half dozen cones before going to work. I just couldn't give up I was addicted, and just haven't been able to give up. I kept saying I need help but I was happy getting stoned and drunk,and when I wasn't I would be un happy. My 40th birthday is coming up soon so I was looking forward to that, I have been enjoying my job as I would drive truck 2 to 3 days a week. Started going to central coast one day sydney. Which would be over night trips,then same thing weekends do the same thing. Get drunk and stoned. I remember one night coming home from the pub,thought I would walk home along the beach. Than walk on footpath not something I done often. I got to the park and saw the slippery dip,that looked good for a rest. So I sat down leaned back and fell asleep. Had no idea how long had been there, and a person was pulling on my arm. I said piss off leave me a loan, then this voice said it's the police. What are you doing he said I'm drunk and needed a rest,and went to sleep. Were do you live he asked in bee street,so they gave me a lift home. That was nice of them I'll stick to the footpath next time. Well it's a week to go before my 40th,bring it on I said. I had a big esky that I bought to hold more beer, so I will be testing it out. I saw a dealer during the week and ask him to hold on to a bag of heads for me. And he said I'll do you a good deal for your birthday so a got 1 once. I arrived at work on the thursday,and boss said I want you to take a load to canberra come back friday. I really didn't want to go but I went, all I could think of was my party. So I took a little bit of heads and papers, to have on trip. Well I've unloaded now to fuel up have some breakfast,and trip back to port stephens. Driving back on the hume high way,there are always the big semi trailers. Flying past me and when empty you need two hands on steering wheel,to stop truck moving about in lanes. Well thats another week over now time for my 40th party saturday night.And I get wasted again,shower get changed then down to the pub for usual friday night. Had 4 beers at home and some cones, I was pressing bottle top lid on my head. And I forgot about it I arrived down the pub,and everyone was laughing at me. I said to the bar maid whats wrong with everyone, she could hardly talk. I went over to table and my friends were all laughing, whats the joke I said. No one would tell me until I went to get another beer, and different bar maid said take that bottle top lid off your head. I forgot all about it.Well that's another night over at pub time for walk home couple more beers and cones then off to bed. I've been thinking for a while now, I'm over this getting drunk and stoned every day. Each day is the same get stoned and drink and get drunk friday saturday nights. It's saturday birthday party day, as I do most saturday morings start drinking and have cones. Went around to mum and dads get eskys ready full of beer's. Sit things up weather was not good was pouring rain,so it's going to be in garage and dad would be cooking on bbq.Well it was starting out to be a great night,friends were turning up and family members. And I had one thing on my mind,I needed to change my life after this night. And I felt this was going to be the last time I got drunk. So I was making sure it would be a great night, the beers were going down well. The picks are always good with beers, mum and dad were doing a great job. The tables were set and the bbq was ready, don't you just love the smell of the cooked steak onions. The food was beautiful great company, then the cake came out. Blow out the candles made a speech,told everyone to enjoy them selfs. The beers were going down well, I said to a work mate those beers have to be finished tonight. It was a good night said to there was 2 beers left,gave him one and I had the last. I was happy they were all gone,people were saying there go byes. I thanked mum and dad for a nice night. Friends wife was giving me a lift home, when I got home I had half a dozen cones went to be. Woke up sunday morning with a shocking hang over. So I made a mix had some cones and breakfast,sat in lounge chair. Thinking about my life and I needed to change,well it was back to work on monday. Its was start of new week rob one of my work mates came over to say hi,and laughed your stoned again yeah. He said again we are praying for you at early morning prayer,I said thanks told him I need help. I'm over the life I have been living,and been thinking about suicide. I have be come fed up everyday, day in and out is the same. Getting stoned drunk when I could. There would not be a day go by were I would not be stoned. As if I had no money I could always get my drugs on credit. That's another weeks work gone,and it's friday night. My dealer I was buying my drugs off,was thinking of seeing him. And ask for some herion to commit suicide. I new there was a better life for me,and new there was a God. And i got down on my knees and cried and cried out too God for help. I had tiers flowing down my face like rivers. And my neighbor was knocking on the door,yelling out are you ok. I went to the door sorry for disturbing you I said I need help. Whats wrong I said need help,she came in told her all about it. I said if it was not my love for my mum and dad, and what it would of done to them knowing there son committed suicide. And I love them so much I know there was a better life. Told her I'm going to church on sunday, I called rob that had been praying for me. Tell him I will be at church on sunday,he said thats great you can sit with us. It was sunday morning I was having second thoughts,no I'm going see what it's like. I arrived out side there was so many people, and I saw rob went in with them. It wasn't to bad rob took me to see the pastor. He was pleased to see me,sit down we sing some songs then he said do a message,then open the altar for prayer. The pastor opened the altar and I went up,I was standing there with all there's other people. I could hear people crying and the pastor praying for them. Someone came up behind me and said extend your arms out while he put his hand on my back.The pastor came to me,and ask me what was wrong. Told him I was sick of life and had thoughts of committing suicide. And said I need help I need a change, he asked if I believed jesus died and rose again,yes he told me was going read the sinners prayer. And I repeat after him and ask if I wanted to be baptised in the Holy Spirit yes. So he was praying and I was crying started to shake,and fell backwards snd hit the floor. I heard this voice what happen pastor said you was touched by the Holy Spirit. I stood up and he gave me a hug,and others came to congratulate me. I felt different then I needed to sit down. And a lady came and said to me now the next step,was to go into the waters of baptism. This was all new to me I said, rob was the pastors name. He arranged for me to see him during the week.I meet the pastor on thursday afternoon after work,he ask me what I thought of church. I enjoyed it told him all my story he spoke to me about the water of baptism. I told him I was still smoking drugs,he said it affects people differently. Some people get delivered from drugs and getting drunk. And others when they go into the water of baptism, get delivered the old is dead the new is born when you come out of the water. A month had past and meet with pastor talk more about my baptism day.said have you been drunk since I was baptised in the holy spirit that was huge for me. As I used to get drunk every week,and I have not been drunk since. My baptism in the holy spirit on my first sunday at church,praise God that my life is changing. I have been enjoying church have meet some nice people. This week I'm to meet with the pastor to talk more about my baptism day. You wouldn't believe it I had come down with bronchitis, I said I still wanted to get baptised on my set day. Pastor said no we will wait until I'm well,ok I said as it was winter at the time. And the water will be like ice,a month had past and I was well again. And the date was set 19th of july 1998,I ask mum and dad would they come. Would make the day all that more special having mum and dad there. The day was fast approaching and I was so looking forward to it,I just new God was going to do a miracle on that day. My life has changed so much, have stopped getting drunk and only been stoned a few times. That is a miracle in it self, I had been telling family and friends about I'm now able to talk in tongues as I have the Holy Spirit dwells with in me. There probably saying he's mad, no just praising God my life is going to change even more. Bring it on I say been counting the days down for my new life to begin, and to be free of drugs and getting drunk. I have 7 days to go and it will be sunday I was so happy. Well its sunday morning a big day for me,and It was freezing still winter and a strong westerly wind blowing.

The pastor had announced that there is a baptism after church today please come down and support phillip. It will be at conroy park I was so excited,rob my work mate he will be coming into the water with me and pastor rob. We had arrived at the beach there was alot from church, and I was so happy that mum and dad were there,I new God was going to do a miracle in me. It was so cold the pastor told me what was going to happen,then the 3 of us started to walk out into the water. They had hold of each arm and down I went under the water. And out again put my arms up in the air,praising God that I was a new person. The old phillip gone the new is born the pastor and rob gave me a hug. Then others were hugging me,and mum and dad. Went to toilet get out of wet cloths, I was so happy a new lease on life. And I never touched the drugs again or got drunk. Praising God that a new person was born,I continued going to church most sundays. 17 years has past and to this day never touched the drugs or got drunk again,praise god only he can do that. Still enjoying church there was so much more,that I could of put in this story. But I felt was best to leave out,I pray that this story will change others. That are experiencing what I went through. 27/09/2015

said, your life is like driving your car at night with the headlights on, you only have to see 200 feet in front of you….and the next 200 feet…and the next 200 feet and so on to get to your destination, you don't have to see the whole journey. To me, that means just taking baby steps in the right direction with what you have from where you are at the time. I'll just keep doing things I enjoy when I can and trust the Universe will get me to my Dharma.

I can honestly say that after this weekend, hearing Anita Moorjani's story and listening to Wayne Dyer speak…I honestly don't care if I lose the money in my account or get it all back and more. Man O Man, if I hadn't grown as much as I have Spiritually over the past few years I would have been suicidal if I made $10,000.00 and lost $7000.00, I hate to think of what the old me would have done, that's a blessing in itself!

I'm just going to do it because I enjoy it, not for any particular outcome and besides, I reached my Goal of $10000.00, (by the way, I have read that when you what to reach a goal, it helps to say at the end…*this or something better*, so you don't restrict the Universe) and we've still got $2000.00 in our holiday account that we didn't have, can't complain about that.

If Day Trading isn't what I'm meant to be doing at the moment, then something else is out there for me when the time is right.

Dr. Dyer read out this great saying by Patanjali
He said-

When you are inspired by some great purpose, some extraordinary project, all your thoughts break their bonds, your mind transcends limitations, your consciousness expands in every direction and you find yourself in a new, great and wonderful world, dormant forces, faculties and talents become alive and you discover yourself to be a greater person by far then you ever dreamed yourself to be.

So, I think I've learnt a great lesson, do something because you love it, not for what you can get out of it, and don't turn interests into a cursed how!!

Wayne Dyer also explained how, in the grand scheme of things, our planet, let alone our physical selves, are a tiny little speck in the Universe, (which we are all connected to) and if you truly believe that you are an eternal spiritual being... (which I have truly come to believe we all are) this life is the blink of an eye. When this life is done, and I know that I am eternal, and a powerful creator, and could have created anything I wanted, am I really going to worry about the little bumps in the road, or am I going to say to myself... *I wish I knew who I was and how powerful I was when I was in that physical body, I would have never worried about little things like that, I would have achieved anything I wanted to...*well, I'm still here!

Talk about thinking from the end!

18

The Great Man

L ast time I wrote in here I was saying what a fantastic weekend we had at the Wayne Dyer Seminar in Brisbane. This morning on the way to town Marina read on Facebook that Wayne Dyer passed away in Maui Saturday night (Maui time).

We are in shock, only a few weeks ago we meant him and shook his hand, he was saying that he hasn't felt better in his life, he seemed so healthy and energetic. Even though we didn't really know him, we feel like we've lost a close friend, Marina actually cried that's the effect this amazing, amazing man had on people. He helped changed so many people's lives and touched millions around the World to say that he is going to missed by millions is an understatement.

This is one of my favorite sayings by the great Man-

When you change the way you look at things, the things you look at change

RIP Dr. Wayne W Dyer.

19

The Day Off

10th September 2015

I had the day off today and I've been feeling a bit flat lately so I thought I'd take Teddy (our fur child) to Colleges Crossing, it's a Nature reserve beside a river and they have picnic areas and a nature walk, just a really nice place.

When I was there watching teddy run through the water and just soaking up nature, I was thinking of the things Wayne Dyer was saying at his Seminar, (I don't want to offend anyone by saying this) but I really felt like he was there with me, and it made me think of how Anita Moorjani said when she was in the other Realm, she felt like her energy could be in a lot of different places at the same time, so I really believe he is with a lot of people, he touched so many.

I was thinking about how he was saying that our spirit is eternal and that we are NOT Human Beings Sometimes Having a spiritual experience, but we are

Eternal, Spiritual beings sometimes having a physical experience. He was also saying that everyone has a Dharma, a divine purpose.

The last few days my job has been getting to me amongst other things, and sometimes I get impatient and frustrated because I just can't seem to find my purpose in life. I've tried to do things that make me happy and things I enjoy doing and waiting for opportunities to arrive that might get me out of what I'm doing and on to my life purpose and just letting things unfold the way their meant to but sometimes, when your caught up in life, and just not happy with the way things are, it's hard to do that, let alone think of all the things I've been trying to put into practice that I've learnt over the years, I just want to find my Dharma!

But then, sitting on that log next to the river watching Teddy, I thought of Wayne Dyer's words...*we are eternal,* and I thought... *really, the only things that matter in this life is the experiences I gain, not the problems or the worries, they'll all go with this life and who I really am will move on with all the experiences I've had in this life and exist for eternity, and probably experience another physical life again sometime with even more experiences so bumps in the road in this life really aren't worth getting upset over.* I'm starting to realize how important thinking and living from your spiritual self and not your physical self is, and I don't mean airy fairy stuff in the sky, or locking yourself away in a monastery somewhere for ten years, I mean putting things in perspective, Spiritual perspective, because that's the real perspective. I stress less and I don't worry about things as much when I take the time to do this, because, like I said before, this life is the blink of an eye, all our problems will vanish with it and I believe the experiences will remain.

So then, I thought, well, what's the point of life? I think the point is to follow and realize your dreams, to experience the ecstasy of achieving a goal and living a happy, blissful life all the time, not just sometimes, living heaven on earth, finding your Dharma. I'm starting to realize that that is what life is about, following your heart and living your dreams, because I don't think I was born to experience struggle, stress, worry disappointment and unhappiness all the time and then die, what's the point of that? why be born at all?

It also makes it easier to understand that we do have the power to create our life the way we want, otherwise there would be no point to life, I don't believe we come here to suffer or experience disappointment and just let life happen to us without having the tools to change the situation that make us uncomfortable, like I said, what would be the point of that? I think problems we come across in our lives are the Universe's tool to keep us on track, to say to us...*Hay, you're getting off track a bit there*! like running over cat's eyes on the road when you start to fall asleep, a temporary wake up call, and all problems are only temporary, no matter how big you think they are; just a shove in the right direction, they can't last forever.

I'm starting to understand how important it is to just separate yourself from your life sometimes, just to put your mind right again. For me, my separation or buffer is Nature, it's like a deep form of meditation for me and that's one blessing that we have had the last few years. Being able to go away for weekends and just enjoy being in nature which would have been imposable for us just a few short years ago because of our financial situation.

I was thinking that I haven't really achieved that much over the past six years, but when I think about it, I have achieved a fair bit, even before I started writing this Journal, before I knew any of this way of thinking or more truthfully, started to remember what my Spirit has always known. Even when people don't realize who they really are, they still achieve things in life. A perfect example is a mate of mine who's a Builder. Even though he is doing pretty well financially, like everyone, he suffered through the Financial crisis but I hardly ever heard him say a negative thing, I think the most negative thing he said was... *"you know mate, I think this is the quietest I've been in 30 odd years"*. But even through those days he would ring me about a plastering job or something else and I'd ask him how he is, and he'd say... *"I woke up this morning mate so that's a good thing"*! And nearly every time I ring him, I ask him how he is and he says... *"I'm bloody fantastic Knoxie, how are you Mate"*?

Now he is so busy he can't keep up with it, just the other day he showed me his missed calls for that day, there was 54 missed calls on his phone which for a small business is a lot, considering through the financial crisis our phones wouldn't ring for sometimes a week or so at a time. As far as I know, he knows nothing about this way of thinking and from what I can see he's still achieved a fair bit in his life just from his positive attitude, so imagine what people could achieve if they woke up to who they really are, imagine the possibilities.

When I started writing this, Marina and I were looking at losing our house, our financial situation was not good to say the least and we were just sick of struggling all the time, but by changing the way we think and by starting to realize who we really are, and doing what we could from where we were, it started to turn our lives around. We are both different people from when we started and in a lot better place. A lot of things have gotten so much better over the past 6 years because of this Spiritual journey that we're both on.

20

My Biggest Challenge

<u>8th October 2015</u>

My biggest challenge in life has been my work life, by far. I was talking to my Mother on the phone just last night and she basically said that most of the grief I've had in my life comes back to work, the jobs I've had, and she's right. Even when it comes to the failed relationships I've had, a lot of the problems came from me being frustrated, angry and depressed and just feeling trapped a lot of the time because of work, not enjoying what I do. I think the closest I've ever been to being content with my job is having a trade and being my own boss, but I'm sure Marina gets sick of me saying... *"I'm frigg'n sick of my job"*!

Sometimes over the years I've thought to myself, *why can't you be like other people you know and just be happy with your job, or at least be content, like they are, just be happy you've got a job, or just be happy you've got a trade and you own your business.* I cover it up pretty well around people most of the time because they would probably think the same things and think, *just be happy with what you're doing*, but I can't, no matter how much self-talk I do, like... *you could be doing a lot worse things in life, you have a trade, you have your own business, you're your own boss...what's wrong with you*! That does work for a little while, but eventually I end up having the same negative feelings.

But from the things I've learnt over the past few years, I think everyone does have a Dharma, a life purpose, something their meant to achieve in their life, and I believe whatever it is, it will not only benefit yourself but also the people around you and I also believe that just by living your Devine purpose, a by- product of that is also living your dream life, because the Universe will open doors and bring things to you because you've found your Dharma. Can you imagine if everyone found their purpose in life which would not only benefit themselves but also the people around them, the Planet would be a much happy place, not to mention your own personnel world.

Maybe I just haven't found my life purpose yet.

I have always had this feeling that I'm meant to do something in life, a certain path I'm meant to follow and that's why I always, eventually, end up getting frustrated, angry and depressed with the jobs I've had because I'm not on the path I'm meant to be on. Then I see some people who are a lot younger then me who seem to have found their passion in life and I think, *maybe it's past me by, I'm 47 now so maybe I just didn't see the signs.* I've tried really hard to be open to signs from the Universe, especially since I've started this journey, and have tried to stay conscious of things that interest and excite me but it hasn't happened yet, work wise anyway.

But then, I do believe in divine timing, it could be that it just hasn't been the right time yet, maybe everything I've experienced so far will one day all come together and I will find my Dharma. The hardest part is being patient, I've never been a patient person, that might be one thing the Universe is trying to get me to work on, if so…enough already!!

21

Devine Purpose

<u>11th October 2015</u>

You know, I have never written anything in my life, I have never even kept a diary even though my Mother use to try an encourage me to when I was younger, so reading back through some of my journal I was thinking...*who wrote this*? It doesn't seem like I wrote it when I read it, and then the thought crossed my mind that maybe my Dharma is staring me in the face, maybe part of my life purpose is to share my journey of slowly waking up to who I really am, of realizing that I am a piece of God, a powerful creator who can make my life the way I want it, after all, there would be so many people out there with a similar story to mine and similar challenges in their life and I have proven to myself that all of this is true, and if it's true for me (and Marina), it's true for everyone, because we all come from the same place, we are all a piece of God...made by, and of God, a part of the Universal energy that runs through everyone and everything in the Universe.

It's an old cliché but I can take the ribbing I'll get from my Mates (who knows, some of them might even start their own Journey of waking up to their selves), if people can get something helpful out of my Journey, that would really be something special.

I've also realized that I actually really enjoy writing and have enjoyed keeping this journal, I think it will be an ongoing thing for me now.

To top it all off, when we were at the Wayne Dyer Seminar in Brisbane, they had a table there with Information about a branch of the Hay House Company called *Balboa Press* which is a self-publishing Company. Marina filled out a form with our email address and our Information on it just to find out what it was about, she only put my name on the form, (bear in mind that Marina didn't know I was keeping this journal). Not long after thinking that maybe part of my life purpose might be to share my Story, I got an email from Alexa from Balboa Press with Information about the Company but also she asked…*Paul, I would be interested to know what your plans are for your book*!!

It amazes me sometimes how the Universe operates. The further we've got into our Spiritual journey, the more frequent these "coincidences" seem to happen.

My youngest Son, Dylan, rang me a few nights ago to have a chat. He finished high school a few year ago and he's been a bit lost, career wise. He's had a few different jobs. He started a painting apprenticeship, his older brother, Blaine, got him a job where he worked and he went to University for a while, but nothing has really sparked any interest or passion.

He has always been a gifted and talented sportsman, whatever sport he's played, he's excelled at but especially golf. My Mother's partner, Russell, put a golf club in his hands when he was about 4 years old, and he could actually hit the ball! Dylan has always had fantastic hand-eye coordination.

He started playing seriously when he was about 8, his Mother got him a membership at their local Golf Club, (he lived with her and I saw him every second weekend and half of all the school holidays) so he had a lot of support from her and I gave him as much support as I could. He started winning tournaments and got a Scholarship to a high school in Brisbane for Golf and was doing really well with it, He always use to tell me that he was going to be a pro Golfer when he grew up and I didn't doubt it because he definitely had the talent. But a few things happened in his life that put him off Golf for a while.

So, the other night when he rang he said- *"you know Dad, I've tried a few different things over the past couple of years and I've tried my best to stick it out, but it just turns into a nightmare, I just can't keep doing it. The only thing I love and am passionate about is Golf, I'm going to pursue my dream."*

I said to him that everyone is born with certain gifts and talents, things that just come natural that I believe your meant to use for your Life purpose, your given those gifts and talents for a reason and yours is sport.

71

Ever since my Sons were little, I always told them that I didn't care what they did in life as a career, as long as they love doing it, as long as Their passionate about it, because if you do that, all the material things will follow.

So I said to Dylan- *"that's great, it's fantastic, follow your dreams, if you follow your passions, you don't know what doors will open for you, I will support you has much as I can."*

My eldest Son, Blaine, loves his job, he done a green keeping apprenticeship at a Golf course after a few dead end jobs after he left School and is now a qualified green keeper. He has just finished working at a Golf course in New York (rent free) for 6 months, he was also given the opportunity to work in England for a while but decided to come back home. He's already got a job at a great Golf club when he gets home.

Now, Blaine didn't finish High School and he is travelling the World with his job. People might say- *well, he's just lucky,* and I say…*no, he loves his job and because of that doors have opened for him, but more than that, he had the courage to walk through those doors when the opportunity's come along.* And they will come along for Dylan as well, and every person who is following their passions, who are following their heart.

If your dream is to go to Uni, and your passionate about it, not because that's what other people want you to do, but because that's what you want to do, that's fantastic, go for it, there's a lot of support out there for people who want to go to Uni.

But I also want to give just as much support to the people who are following their passions that might not involve Uni. If you don't go to Uni, or even if you didn't finish High School, it's not the end of the world, there are so many very successful people in the World that didn't go to Uni and didn't finish High School.

When your lost and just don't know what to do anymore, follow your heart, follow your interests and passions, even if it's not a *"real job"* and doors will open up for you, you will find your path to your Devine purpose in life, your Dharma, just don't give up, keep your dreams alive, it will happen.

If you're in your 30's, 40's, 50's, 60's, 70's, or whatever decade you're in, re-kindle those dreams, those interests and passions, you don't have those dreams, interests and passions for no reason, and they don't stay with you during your life for no reason either, give them the attention and time they deserve, there your gifts from the Universe to follow.

Louise Hay started her very successful Company-*Hay House* when she was in her 60's, what an inspiration.

You don't know what doors the Universe will fling open for you to walk through by following you heart, and the Universe doesn't care about your age, whether you finished High School, whether you went to University or where you came from, once again, there physical insecurities, insecurities of the ego. Source energy just wants for you want you want for yourself, to be happy and abundant in all areas of life, that's our birthright, to live heaven on earth, as above, so below, all you have to do is have the courage to grab those opportunities the Universe sends you and walk through those doors when they open.

22

The Real Me

In hindsight, it makes sense now that a big part of my Dharma is writing. When I think about when I was younger and also throughout my life, I have always been an arty type person. When I was young I use to spend hours upon hours drawing and painting cartoons, it was my favorite past time. I have also been a thinker; I spend a lot of time thinking about numerous different things.

That's my personal side, the real me, the side most people didn't see. Most of the people around me seen the sporty me, the me that loved going out with his mates, getting drunk and having a good time, the me I showed people because that's who I thought they would like. Although I did enjoy those things when I was younger, it wasn't who I really was. The real person I am is an arty thinker who enjoys spending time in nature and thinking about the Spiritual side of things and the mysteries of life.

Writing is an art form and I believe people who spend a lot of time thinking should write their thoughts down, you don't have a lot of thoughts and spend time thinking about numerous different things for no reason, and the 30 odd years' experience of not liking what I did in my work life has given me plenty of things to write about and share with others. It has also given me the understanding and empathy for people who haven't found their Dharma yet, people who don't want to get out of bed in the morning because they hate the thought of going to work! And it has given me the motivation to help them because I know what it's like to not enjoy your work life, it can be a living nightmare!

So, what type of person are you? the real you, not the public you, not the you that all your friends see, the real you. Are you arty? Are you a thinker? Do you think a lot about numerous different things? Do you like using your hands, building things? Are you sporty? Do the mysteries of the world interest you? Are you a combination of some or maybe all of these thing?

That personal you is who you really are, the person you may not let many other people see. I tell you now, that person will give you clues as to what your Devine purpose is in this life. Be proud of it, of who you really are, follow it, if you lose friends because of being who you really are, then their purpose in your life has been fulfilled, let them go and move on to your purpose in life. Be who you really are, you won't find your Dharma, (and as a consequence of finding your divine purpose), live your dream life, any other way.

Over the years, accepting, acknowledging and honoring who I really am has been life transforming, it has let me discover my Dharma and in a few short weeks my interest in sharing my journey in the hope it will help and inspire others find their Dharma has turned into a passion- an obsession (in a good way).

I've found my Devine purpose, now I want to help others find theirs.

23

The Gift Of Experience

<u>21st October 2015</u>

It turns out that all the feelings of frustration, depression and feelings of feeling trapped over the last 30 odd years due to my work life was actually the gift of experience! All those times I woke up wishing I didn't, those thoughts that I was having a crappy life because of bad Karma, thinking I have to pay the Universe back for some miss deed in a past life, of thinking...*why are you doing this to me God!!* was all a Devine gift of experience. Because of that experience, I can now share it with other people who are going through the same thing in their work life, more importantly I understand how they are feeling and by sharing my journey I can help and hopefully inspire them to find their Devine purpose in life, their Dharma.

The Universe new what it was doing all along; giving me the experience I needed to share with other people so I could help them find their own Devine purpose. The big message in this is never...never ever give up! I'm 47 years old and I've only just found my Dharma. Now, instead of waking up wishing I didn't, I wake up so excited about writing and sharing my journey with other people and as a consequence, helping people find their Devine purpose.

Source energy truly does use people for a Devine purpose, it uses people as a tool to help others in their journey through this planet and as a byproduct of living your Dharma, you start living your dream life because you are on the path Source wants you to be on, the path you were born for, the Devine purpose you were sent here for to help others.

Now, to find my Dharma in life isn't just my reason for being here in this physical body, or for this person or that person, it's not just for the privileged people to find or the people who have had a lot of struggle in their lives, or for people who have a particular religious belief, a certain astrological chart, or whatever excuses you can think of as to why you're not living your dream life yet… yes…YET! It is for every single person on this planet to find their Devine purpose in life, no matter who you are or where you come from, so you can help others and as a consequence, live your dream life because when your living your Dharma, the Universe supports you, everything goes right in your life, things you need, the Universe will bring to you, exciting new doors will open for you to go through, all because you are doing what Source energy wanted for you before you came into this physical time and space World, and also what you wanted for yourself.

All these things are just starting to happen to me, and whatever anyone's Dharma is, you can be sure the result of following it will help other people, especially the people around you. If everyone on this planet were living their life purpose, can you imagine what the world would be like, it would be heaven on earth, they would all feel the excitement you will feel every day when you find your Dharma.

So, whatever you do, no matter how old or young you are or the circumstances your now in or what other people say...don't ever...ever give up, the Universe needs you, and so do other people. You are Source energy in physical form, you are Source's eye's, hands and ears. Like I said, every single person was sent here to find their Dharma, not just the lucky few...don't give up, if you give up, you can't help the people you were sent here to help.

When I say help, it's not just a physical thing, it could be that the paintings you paint make people feel good, it could be the poems you create make people feel loving, it could be a book you write will inspire people, it might be that the money you make when you find your Dharma will help people who need financial help, or, it might be physical, you might be a builder and build someone's dream home...you might build a lot of dream homes for people, you might be a Traddie who works on these dream houses to help bring them into the owner's reality. The only important thing is, you have to love what you do, you have to be passionate about it, if you're not, more than likely, it's not what you were born to do, it's not your Dharma.

79

Keep trying different things that excite you, try new experiences when they show up in your life, walk through doors that the Universe opens for you, but don't turn them into a cursed how. You don't know which of these interest the Universe will use to put you on your path to your Devine purpose. Eventually you will find your Dharma. It could be that your biggest challenge in your life might have something to do with your Devine purpose, embrace your circumstances and your challenges in life, they could be valuable tools to use when you find your Dharma, which will always be in Devine time.

My biggest challenge in life - my work life, turned out to be my most important and valuable gift from the Universe, those experiences and challenges had everything to do with my life purpose, my Dharma, and even though it seemed to take forever, and I got so impatient and frustrated a lot of the time, and just didn't want to get out of bed to face the day, it all happened when it was meant to, in Devine time, things wouldn't be the way they are if it was any earlier or any later...all in Devine time.

I've been on this Spiritual journey for 7 years now, so it's taken awhile to find my Devine purpose in life, my Dharma, and when I was in the thick of it, it felt like an eternity, but I remember reading something in one of Mike Dooley's books which said something like this- just keep going, keep trying from where you are, with what you have and always and only keep focused on the end result of what you want to achieve, not the how's, not the whys, not the when's, not the doubts that you can't do it, just what it will feel and look like when you've achieved your goal like it's already achieved, and don't give up, keep going, it will all happen in Devine time. After a while, you will reach critical mass, a point of no return, the flood gates will start to open, and your life will, (at first), start to trickle and then the gates will fly open and your life will take off!

When you really think about life, how amazing is it. Source energy gave us physical life from itself, we are God in physical form which gives us all the power we need to create. It gave us free will to choose whatever our heart desires to experience, it gave us dominion over all things so we can bring the experiences we want into our lives, whatever they are (*dominion over All Things!*) and to top it all off, we are eternal so there's no reason to fear anything, who we really are never dies. Man O man, how amazing is life!

But the reason there's so much suffering in the world, is because most people haven't woken up to themselves, they don't understand or believe in who they really are; a piece of God, Source energy in physical form with all the power they need to create whatever they want. Without belief, all the power in the Universe means nothing, it all means nothing without belief...You got to believe!

Marina and I have both grown so much, spiritually over the past seven years and because of that we can never go back to who we were, our lives have changed so much for the better because of our Spiritual growth, but this isn't the end, it is only just the start, things can only get better from here! The more we grow Spiritually, the more we wake up to ourselves... to who we really are, the better our lives will get... and so will yours if you start to discover and start believing in who you really are, I know that now for sure!

I better write an Introduction for my journal and send it to Alexa and see where it takes us

On with the Journey!

Notes

Notes

Notes

Notes

Notes

Printed in the United States
By Bookmasters

least many of them are still helping God in their everyday lives. Values education in our schools must be having some effect, inadequate as it may be in settling multi-cultural disputes, or if students see it as no more than school rules to be left behind at the school gates. Most teachers are sincerely doing their best, but It will take a great deal to convince today's masses of educated people that their enemy is not other people, other races or other religions, or any religion, but the force of evil working on their minds.

19

MORE EFFORTS TO COMMUNICATE WITH THE CHURCH

In May 2007 a questionnaire was sent to Parish vestries and Clergy in New Zealand. A Draft Covenant was circulated widely for study and the questionnaire was asking for submissions. At the time, I wrote in my diary that it seemed the church was worried about divisions and was not sure which way to go. -

"Another of evil's little tricks is to confuse us, getting us running this way and that, all in order to distract us from God's purpose for the world. It seems that I have to communicate with the church again. I am to tell them that they are to allow another branch of the Christian church to grow up alongside the old. They are not to try to destroy each other, but need to grow alongside each other. God himself will choose which branch will survive. Evil of course will try to convince them to fight against each other – all in the name of Jesus Christ. Will they listen to God or Evil?"

Submissions were to be sent in time for discussion here in New Zealand in 2007 and in the U.K. in July 2008, so I sent my comments but I have never had a reply. Should I have expected anyone to answer what I wrote? Back in the Middle Ages, I would probably have been burned at the stake. I had been told that if the church would not listen to me I should go to the people, so now several years on, I am writing here for the wandering flock who have probably not been particularly concerned about what is happening within the churches, so a little background information is required for them. Not too much because this is what the manuscript assessor warned me could be boring for them.

Much of what I included in my submission has already been written here, about Jesus, about the church needing to offer alternative beliefs, to let two branches grow and not to fight against each other.

There were also statistics showing that the numbers attending mainline churches are declining and comments on what is happening. The growing churches are either explicitly Pentecostal, or heavily influenced by charismatic practices. [32] There was my belief that unless Jesus is accepted as a man and not as part of God, there will never be acceptance of God as an umbrella over all mankind.

I went on to point out that **The emphasis of the charismatics had been on the "Baptism of the Holy Spirit"** which they claimed, would bestow on those who asked, gifts that would enable them to serve Jesus. Most of the charismatics were very sincere people who

---

[32] Noll, M. (1997) 2nd ed. 2000. *Turning points: Decisive moments in the history of Christianity.* USA : Baker Academic. P 300.

have gone on faithfully serving and teaching in a way that many members of mainstream churches would not be prepared to do.

I wrote that in all my years within the Church before the 1970s when the charismatic movement was introduced locally, I had heard no mention of any intense religious experience. I had however heard in the 1930s of the "Blessing of the Holy Spirit" as it was called then. It had been described to us by our Presbyterian "Crusader" leader at secondary school, as an intense experience of love that enabled those on whom it was bestowed, to be completely convinced of the existence of God. I stated that such words would not have been used in the 1930s, but today the experience could be described as a spiritual orgasm, an experience that gave the recipients the courage and power to go out and spread His word. As it was explained to us in the thirties by our leader, who had experienced this blessing herself, it is not given merely for the asking. Only when our cup was completely emptied of self could it be filled with the Holy Spirit. I stated that I believed it was probably the experience of the apostles on the day of Pentecost, the experience that had enabled them to leave their room and go out and speak the good news, and that though they spoke in languages that could be understood by the variety of people present at the time, as Paul said later, (1Corinthians 12:30) not everyone would receive the same gifts or speak in strange tongues. I wrote, "It is probably fair to say, that in the 1960s and 1970s we were given a sample of the power of the Holy Spirit that could be made available to us when we could be trusted to use it in the way that God demands – to teach His word, to teach the truth, and to offer it in a way that is relevant to the educated masses of to-day. It is also fair to say that we "blew" that opportunity - but the offer is still open."

Public exhibitions of emotion however are not commonplace in a mainstream church. Here, in the 1970s, they were regarded by many people with suspicion and disapproval. During a church service we do not wave our arms around and shout "Praise the Lord."

I quoted one writer, "The real strength of Anglicanism has remained in the quiet ordinariness of communal parochial life – in the peace engendered by the beauty of simple worship – the dedicated labours of parochial clergy and the often unacknowledged devotion of the ordinary men and women in the pew."[33] "There has also been an intellectual respectability with Anglicanism that is not given to churches that are noted for their extreme behaviour, but the search for and experience of an ecstatic religious experience may help to explain the rapid growth of the Pentecostal churches."[34] I suggested that if the traditional strengths of a mainstream Church could be combined with the evangelical power that could be made available through the "Blessing of the Holy Spirit," there could be new life and hope for the Church, and that by offering the power to mainline churches at the beginning of this present movement, it seemed that God has shown that He wants it to be in responsible hands.

I wrote that though it was not spelled out in the proposed Covenant, the issues of women and homosexuals in the clergy, seemed to be the issues that were of most concern and were causing division, but to me they were not the most important if the church was to survive. In my submission to the questionnaire in 2007 I wrote that -

"The question we need to ask now, and the most important issue that will influence our decisions is this – What is more important, the

---

[33] Green, V., (1996). Chapter 11: 'The Crisis of the modern Church' (p351) in *A new history of Christianity.*

[34] Ibid p 371

traditions and institution of the Church, or that the message brought to us by Jesus Christ himself should reach the people for whom it was intended? Any form of systematic academic research will go back to the source documents rather than depending on later interpretations. Jesus himself is the source document of Christianity. He considered God as his Father, and he taught righteousness and a way of life. His followers at first were called followers of 'The way.'"

The draft document had stated that the church was committed to a pilgrimage with other members of the Communion to discern truth, "that peoples from all nations may truly be free and receive the new and abundant life in the Lord Jesus Christ."

I asked whether we were being told here that people from all nations would need to become Christians according to the Creed that we say, or whether it was God's intention that people of all nations will see themselves as one family with one Father God, and accept the teaching of Jesus as a messenger of God

"We have a God who insists on truth. A Christianity that will survive into the future and thrive as a major force in the world, must be acceptable to reason as well as to faith." Were they really seeking the truth?

Then finally in my submission I wrote -

"There have been many places in the history of Christianity that have been regarded as turning points or decisive moments. If Christianity survives as a major force in the world, future generations may see decisions made at this time by the ------ Church as one of these decisions. A new version of Christianity is required now, based on the knowledge we have and the needs of to-day's society. If we are to believe John's Gospel, one of the last requests of Jesus was, 'Feed my sheep.' It was made three times, as if Jesus knew he was asking a great deal of Peter. Any farmer knows that it is useless to offer food to an animal in a form it distrusts and will not eat, and so it is with the message of Christianity for today.

. As large institutions, mainstream churches do need considerable organization, but the institutions as they have grown over the years, should never become more important than the message they were formed to promote."

There was never any reply to these submissions.

Out of all this in 2013 there came the knowledge that I had to send this book when it is finished to the Roman Catholic Church also. I have sent the first version to them, the version named "In the beginning," that was compiled for the Church, but now I am revising that book for the wandering flock who need a slightly different version. Back in the early days of my journey I wrote, "Have our priests given up hope?" If they believe me, it will prove to them that God is not dead. He is not a delusion. He has tried to communicate with His Church. It is not His fault if the Church does not recognize his voice.

Speaking for myself, I can only ask how does anyone think God could or would give a message to the Church today? Is He going to send a meteor with a letter on it? What would happen if a prophet He had sent, stood on a street corner and shouted warnings to the public? The Roman Catholic Church is said to have the keys of the Kingdom. Could a new Pope become the one to unlock the door?

20

REASON

C an we accept that reason and truth need to be the basis for any ethical code that could be accepted as a "Global Ethic" for the future? My experience at University has shown me that no one particular religion is going to be accepted as the ultimate authority. Religion itself is not going to be accepted. The "ongoing conversation" will continue, It should not be too difficult for open-minded people to accept that even if human reason alone were the source, there are similarities in the ethical teachings of most main religions that indicate that reason and logic led the thinkers – the prophets, shamans and philosophers - along the same lines. Educated masses need reason and logic, not just faith and obedience. However as Ninian Smart wrote - [35]

"No-one can understand mankind without understanding the faiths of humanity."

---

[35] Ninian Smart (1971) *The religious experience of mankind.* P 664

When we go back to the source documents of all the main religions we find much similarity in ethical teachings, though I did not discover this until twenty years later when I went back to University to study world religions. In the beginning, my work was to be within the mainly Christian society where I lived. I was shown that God is an umbrella over all mankind. Different groups had spread over the world, and due to the different conditions under which their races evolved, their ideas about the force that communicated with their prophets and their wise men and women had also evolved in different ways. Socrates had his daimon, a divine voice that warned him against wrong actions. Zoroaster saw life as a continuing battle between good and evil. In the Navaho Indian culture of the United States a Holy Wind acted as a messenger wind, warning people of dangers and discouraging them from pursuing certain paths. Their Holy Wind did not punish, but individuals suffered the natural consequences of their own actions.[36] The Proverbs in the Bible are very similar to many of the writings from ancient Egypt that show the same ethical principles.

Thousands of years ago a famous Egyptian inscription called "The Book of the Dead" spelt out a long list of declarations of innocence that the deceased should be able to make. They were very explicit, and very similar to what a majority today would also consider ethical.

– e.g. I have not committed crimes against people.

I have not cheated in land transactions.

I have not added to the weight of the balance.

I have not tampered with the scales.

I have not stolen.

---

[36] Hinman p 81-82

I have not been covetous.

I have not gossiped.

I have not robbed the poor.

I have not discriminated against anyone.

When the Grand Vizier, the CEO of Ancient Egypt, was installed into the office by the King, he was instructed to be fair – giving every man his just deserts – for practical reasons. The CEO is in public view and his office is "The supporting post of the entire land."[37] But behind the practical reasons is also the responsibility to the god Amon-Re, the protector of the poor man, who demands that the official should operate in terms of justice and need rather than law and property.

God spoke to the prophets of Israel and made Muhammad His messenger to Islam. Buddha experienced nirvana when his mind was emptied of self, very much like the Christian Blessing of the Holy Spirit - even though he would not have given credit to any force outside his own mind. Confucius set standards for the "upright" man. The "Chuntzu" would take as long to decide what was right as another man might take to decide what would pay. The stories that the prophets told of the source of their messages are too similar for them to be dismissed by reasonable people, even though the interpretations of the source varied according to the tradition of different cultures.

God has possibly sent other prophets since Muhammad, but they have not been recognized or accepted – and I must not stray into other peoples' fields. I was told that God had other lamps burning under other bushels, but my work was within my own society. I was

---

[37] *The Intellectual adventures of Ancient man.* P 89. University of Chicago Press. 1977 edition

shown that the Christian Church had also evolved and changed from the original teachings. In the 1970s, there was much talk within the charismatic movement of going back to the original Christian church that had emerged after the death of Jesus, but the original message really was what Jesus himself had taught, rather than what had evolved later. The original message was God the Father, and a way of life. The original followers were followers of "The Way," but the apostles had tried to find explanations for what had happened and so the teaching widened.

Councils decided on dogma and produced creeds by way of explanation, far beyond the new commandment that Jesus had given. The God I came to know was the same God who had communicated with all branches of mankind from the beginning. This God was a loving, wise and just Father God who had no favourites amongst His children. They were all equally precious to Him and Jesus himself had said, "In my Father's house there are many mansions.".

Most cultures have developed their own traditions of the origins of mankind. The well-known story of Adam and Eve and the Garden of Eden, was the tradition of the Israelites and was accepted because it was there in the earliest writings. For those of today who cannot accept this as literal truth, the truth is still there in parable form. God gave us a beautiful world and through our own actions we are in danger of destroying it. God will not punish us, but will let us learn by suffering the natural consequences of our own actions. We try to pass the buck to other people. When God asked Adam why he ate the forbidden fruit, Adam produced the common answer, "It wasn't my fault," and then, "The woman tempted me." The story continues that God then told them that their days of leisure were over, and in their future, they would have to work to gain a living. "By the sweat of your brow you will earn your bread." Even the story of the brothers Cain and Abel that follows the expulsion from the Garden of Eden can be seen as a parable. Cain kills Abel and when God asks him where his brother is, Cain replies, "How do I know? Am I my brother's keeper?" So it is today when part of the world wastes food and other parts starve. If we turn a blind eye and say, "It is nothing to do with me," we are playing the part of Cain again. From the beginning of creation it seems that God has been working through evolution to create a species that will be able to communicate with him, listen to Him and live peacefully in the beautiful world that He provided as our environment.

The force of Evil has always been trying to prevent this. It was pictured as the snake in the Garden of Eden offering immediate delicious rewards. In more scientific terms, I read once, (Reader's Digest Encyclopedia) that there had been an early type of ape that seemed to have a ceremony or liking for eating the brains of its victims. To me, it seemed that this was an effort by the force of evil to destroy the possibility of the human brain developing – as though evil knew that the developing human brain was its worst enemy. Darwin and Huxley believed that the morality of mankind would also evolve in a higher direction, but so far the modern human brain does not seem to be moving completely towards its potential for good. The things to which evil keeps drawing our attention are brighter and more attractive at first sight. Individualism and ethical egoism are more attractive short-term than self- sacrifice and the common good – and yet the good is still there. We see it every day in the good things many people do. We just need to clear away the weeds that evil sows, and perhaps our fingers will need to be burned a bit before we will be prepared to listen to God. Those who have heard of

Kohlberg[38] and his theory of ethical reasoning will recognise his lowest level of reasoning - when we will only try to be good because we will suffer personally if we don't. At higher levels, according to Kohlberg, we develop our own standards, moving up from, "Well, everybody does it," to a higher level where our actions are based on our own freely chosen ethical principles, and because of the effect of our actions on other people and the environment. God does not use His power to force us to be good.

Philosophers like Jean-Paul Sartre believe that humans must face up to the absence of God and accept as a fact that human ethical values are not given from outside, but must be created by man, and that humans make up their own character and morality as they go along. [39] Many modern agnostics believe vaguely in a power beyond themselves, but are not convinced that the formal worship of such a Being is important. They are not atheists, but are more against formal religions, than against a belief in an undefined spiritual force. Such people well outnumber the committed atheists of the world. Committed atheists like Karl Marx have had influence well beyond their numbers, and Richard Dawkins, who proclaims that God is a delusion, must be having a considerable influence in our own times with his books and lectures.

Though in the past most children grew up within an environment of religious allegiance of some kind, now many are brought up without religious instruction of any kind, and many others are taught that religion is dangerous and evil.[40] Some of the established religions

---

[38] Kohlberg, L. (1976) The cognitive-developmental approach to moral education. Ch 12 in Purpel and Ryan(eds)
Moral education : It comes with the territory.

[39] Smart. N., (1971) The religious experience of mankind. P 664

[40] ibid p 670

do little to dispel these ideas, though if we look behind the religious inter-fighting it is possible to see the force of evil constantly offering glittering prizes of power and prestige to the leaders, who then use their religions as an excuse to grasp the trophies evil offers, regardless of the cost to other human beings.

In spite of the perceived deficiencies of established religions, humans still seem to have a spiritual need. Today there is a movement by those who cannot accept the concept of a God external to human beings, to make Nature the God. They see humans and nature as an entity. Gaia the Earth Mother figures largely in such thinking, while the Father, God, is eliminated in the process. Many who have no belief in God as He is presented by various religions find a spiritual experience in the beauty of nature and believe that is sufficient, but like any well-balanced family, both mother and father are needed to reproduce and nurture their progeny. Mother Nature may provide our environment, but she does not care about us as individuals. Species evolve or become extinct as their environment changes. Through my experience so far, I know that God cares about all his creation and about every individual, the good and the not so good. Mother Nature on the other hand is unlike our ideal of a human mother. On her own, she would not see the human species as any more important than any other species. If we were to pollute beyond repair, the type of environment that humans need if they are to survive, other species would emerge. They would evolve through their ability to survive in the polluted environment that had led to the demise of humans.

Maybe there are other stars in our skies that were once worlds like ours, but which their inhabitants had polluted beyond recovery. Infinity makes such things possible. Father God has infinite patience, infinite love, infinite power, but He is also wise and just. He gave us free will and we are going to have to make our own choices. God advises us and makes suggestions, but He does not compel us to choose wisely. Accidents of Nature happen, earthquakes, volcanoes erupting, storms and floods, and many humans are injured and people say, "If there is a loving God how can He allow such things to happen?" but we bring most harm on ourselves by the choices we make. If we choose to live at the foot of an active volcano, that is our choice. If we choose to live on an obvious flood-plain, that is our choice. If we choose greed, selfishness and individualism ahead of the common good, that is our choice also. We could evolve into the species God planned from the beginning, or Earth could become another burnt-out planet that scientists will view from afar and say, "We believe there was once human life there." When it comes to human beings, there is one flaw there that prevents us accepting Darwin's theory of evolution completely. If it is totally a matter of "survival of the fittest", the law of the jungle would prevail. Even Dawkins admits that the natural urge of humans to be kind is a "Darwinian mistake."

Everything I have written here so far has been part of introducing God to the masses, so how well have I achieved my purpose? How do I rate for reason and logic?

I maintain God is the force for good in the world. He is invisible, but so is electricity and magnetism. We know they are there by the things they do. We visualize God in human form, but that is natural because we have no other way to visualize Him. Humans are arrogant if they think they can define God. He is not limited by the extent of human capabilities of imagination, and so He can be to us whatever we, as individuals need him to be. He is a presence and a force and once in a vivid dream I saw Him as a dark figure on a throne, surrounded by such a vivid light that I could not bear to keep my gaze on Him. He is completely awe-inspiring, but also a good friend.

The fact that God or "the force for good" as I would describe Him can be seen both as a God of love and the awe-inspiring and seemingly cruel God of the Old Testament is quite understandable to me. A God of love cares about all people and He cares about righteousness because when we act in an unrighteous way we hurt other people. Righteousness is all about the effect of our actions on other people and our environment. Primitive people reasoning at the lowest level ethically would only be concerned about, "Will we be punished if we do this?" or "We won't do that because we know we will be hurt if we do." Are we really any different today? What will it take to make the majority of us care about the effects of our actions on our environment and on future generations? Will we have to suffer personally in our own time or will the welfare of our own grand-children and their children be sufficient motivation to set us on "the paths of righteousness"?.

Scientists may say that there is no proof of a Supreme being or Creator, but it is unscientific to ignore evidence, simply because it does not reinforce our own arguments. "Millions of lives producing millions of words of recorded testimony have borne witness that through religion people experience a power which produces not only righteousness, but also love, joy and peace."[41]

"Religious believers and even religiously minded atheists do experience visions or ecstacies which are extremely hard to define or assess – and which it is unscientific to deny." (ibid p53)

---

[41] Edwards, D. 1969. *Religion and change*. London: Hodder and Stoughton. P35.

Buddha experienced his "Nirvana," even though he did not believe in a God or a soul, but his teaching of righteousness compares very well with "Christian" ethics, which of course, are not exclusive to Christians.

In many primal religions there has been a belief in a supreme being, who has made everything and who at a distance sees everything that goes on amongst them, sometimes disapproving but not often interfering.[42] In many Primal religions it is also very easy to see the power of the force of evil pretending to be a god, and a god who punishes if it is offended, or if traditions are not upheld. Sacrifices must be made to appease it and often the sacrifice is required to be human.

A study of world religions shows that many religions involve the same battle between good and evil, between light and darkness.

The place and date of Zoroaster's birth is uncertain, but is suggested to be somewhere in southern Iran or Afghanistan, between 1000 B.C.E. and 600 B.C.E. Like Buddha, the tradition is that he left home as a youth to seek answers to his deepest religious questions, but after his own religious experience, he arrived at a different answer from Buddha with regard to the source of righteousness. He taught that there was a supreme god, Ahura Mazda, and that moral law requiring human righteousness proceeded from this one good god. This one true god had called him to be a prophet and teach the true religion in which the Supreme God of right or truth is opposed by "The lie." "It was perhaps Zoroaster's cardinal moral principle that each human soul is the seat of a war between good and evil."[43]

---

[42] Noss, D. and Noss, J. 1994. *A history of the world's religions,* New York: Macmillan. P16

[43] (ibid. p393)

It is claimed by those who do not believe in an exterior force, that such emphasis on righteousness is merely the expression of the highest ideals of mankind itself. Primitive people, they claim, had to invent a god to frighten the members of their society into behaving for the common good, but the stories of the prophets who claim to have been conscripted and sent as messengers have too many similarities for an open-minded scientist to ignore.

Possibly the latest successful attempt to communicate through a prophet resulted in the Baha'i Faith. Their belief is that Baha'u'llah was the latest in a line of messengers from God that includes Abraham, Krishna, Moses, Buddha, Zoroaster, Christ and Muhammad. They maintain that there is only one God - that all the world's religions represent one changeless and eternal Faith of God, and that all humanity is one race, destined to live in peace and harmony[44]. Baha'u'llah was not accepted by the faithful of Islam any more than he would be by fundamentalist Christians., and it will be interesting to see what happens within this faith in the future. When religions set their beliefs in stone, those who want to change or add to them in future times and in the light of further scientific information, are cast out. Once established, religions do not see knowledge of God as an endless scroll, that keeps a record, but can also adapt and adjust and enlarge with changing times. It is understandable of course that the Institutions that grow up around the teachings of each prophet believe they must keep the message pure. They have the best of intentions.

---

[44] From *The Baha'is*, produced and distributed by the Baha'li Publishing Trust of the United Kingdom, 6. Mount Pleasant, Oakham, Leicestershire, LE156HU U.K.

21

"THE GOD DELUSION"

I enjoyed reading and commenting on Richard Dawkins' book, "The God Delusion." On the cover it is stated that Dawkins was recently voted one of the world's top three intellectuals, and I wonder if some of that vote reflected a world-wide increasingly negative attitude towards religion. In "The God Delusion" Dawkins makes some very valid comments about organised religion and some of the teachings of religions. He is right in many ways, but to me, he is not right when he says God is only a delusion. I see Dawkins as one of those people who actually know God, but doesn't recognise him as that person he sees regularly in the street. He states that without religions there would have been no Crusades, no witch hunts, no Irish troubles, no suicide bombers, no "shiny-suited bouffant-haired televangelists fleecing gullible people of their money," and he is right, but by inventing such weapons as swords and gun-powder, and modern methods of mass destruction, science has brought as much suffering into the world as religion ever has.

The effects of both science and religion depend on the people who use them. People motivated by greed, envy, hatred and even apathy or laziness, can deliberately make choices that harm others. Sometimes choices that have been made for good reasons have harmful consequences further down the track. Leaders use religion to influence followers for good or evil. People use science to invent new mind-bending and addictive drugs. Dawkins quotes Einstein as saying that he (Einstein) did not believe in a personal God, but also quotes him as saying that, "science without religion is lame but religion without science is blind."[45] Dawkins quotes Einstein's own words, "If something is in me that can be called religious, then it is the unbounded admiration for the structure of the world as far as science can reveal it."

Many of the educated masses of today will feel the same.

Religion, used unwisely, has brought pain and suffering to many, but secular faiths, like Communism and Naziism, and modern weapons of science have brought more deaths than religion. If recent research is to be believed, Communism was responsible for 70 million deaths in Maoist China alone.[46] Science has learned a great deal over the last hundred years but research goes on and scientists hope to learn more. New thinking about established religions however can be met with resistance. There are so many points on which I agree with Dawkins, but God as a delusion is not one of them. Dawkins criticised a writer who did not want to destroy the faith and hope of some fellow human beings.[47] Dawkins saw this as intellectual and moral cowardice. I believe that fear of destroying faith and hope is a reason why so many

---

[45] *The God Delusion* p15

[46] Jung Chang. (2005) *Mao: The unknown Story.* Jonathan Cape.

[47] *The God Delusion* p 17

in the established church do not want to admit to any faults in their beliefs or creeds. I do not want to destroy faith and hope either, but what I have learned is that the truth as it has been shown to me does not destroy faith in God. It may destroy faith in some of the teachings of the church, but for me, the truths that I was shown strengthened a faith that could not accept some of the things I was expected to believe. It will offer faith and hope to many more who cannot accept the picture of God and Jesus that is presented in the teachings of the established churches, or as it is used to encourage martyrdom, cruelty and violence in the name of Allah, or any other religion.

The Enlightenment of the 18th century had the effect that many of the best brains of that time and since, have rejected religion. Many of these thinkers believed that through reason alone, human morality would evolve to produce a better world. This does not appear to have happened, and there could still be much to learn about the unseen force that so many people have believed has communicated with humankind, and has tried to guide humans onward and upward. Religions will not know this for sure if they are unwilling to examine themselves in a scientific manner, and people like Dawkins have been needed to bring the subject into the open for discussion. I heard an eminent scientist say in a T.V. interview, "Science is about reducing uncertainty – not about producing certainty." Science itself may have hold of only part of the truth so far, and often some of the most well-known of scientists dispute each others findings. Science is not infallible.

I read "The God Delusion" with considerable interest. As I read, I made notes commenting on Dawkins' arguments. I filled nearly two exercise books with what I saw as logical counter-argument based on my own experiences, but there is no space for all that here, and

I have to keep reminding myself of my instructions, "No-one is to be criticized or condemned, but the truth must be told." Looking at Dawkins in the light of ethical principles, I felt he was achieving reasonable standards in the "Truth" department, but was lighter in the areas of "Justice" and "Love." As for wisdom, he is considered by many to be one of the great thinkers of our day, so his conviction that God is a delusion must be based on the evidence as he sees it. He writes what he believes to be the truth, but perhaps he has not seen all the truth yet. The force of evil pretending to be God can seem very reasonable at times - as I learned to my own cost. Dawkins' conviction that God is only a delusion reminds me of the time when I was so deceived into thinking that I was doing what God wanted. There is much in his writing that shows that Dawkins has a good heart.

Some of the comments I made in my notes are appropriate here.

Page 178 – Dawkins is very knowledgeable but I feel he is inclined to be biased in his arguments. For instance on page 266 he states that "good historians don't judge statements from past times by the standards of their own," and yet he goes back to the Old Testament of the Bible for some of his comparisons. If we ignore the bits of history that don't suit us we are deceiving our readers just as much as priests are, who are teaching their followers things that they don't believe themselves. I believe he is right in his resume of Christian dogma, but that is not all there is to Christianity. At first the Gentiles (non-Jews) were attracted to the teaching because it taught a way of life, and they were attracted to the ethical side of it. It was even called "The Way" at times. Looking at Paul's[48] letters in the New Testament of the Bible, it

---

[48] Paul was a highly educated Jew who was persecuting the new Christians, until on his way to Damascus, he had an experience that convinced him that Jesus was truly a messenger from God. Then he became a leader in taking the

pays to check to whom he was writing. Any good teacher adapts his style of teaching to his audience. Trying to explain the unexplainable to other teachers would require a different style from explaining a "way of life" to the ordinary people. The mythology came in later centuries as others tried with human reason to explain what Jesus and the disciples had experienced.

The message would still appeal to the masses now if the Christian church could lift Jesus up as a man who was prepared to be nailed to the cross because of his belief in the force that had communicated with him and given him work to do. In the same way the disciples experienced this force for themselves on the day of Pentecost. They then had the courage to go out into their world and talk about it. And so did Paul, who had been persecuting Christians or Followers of The Way, as they were known then. Dawkins is a scientist. It would take courage for a scientist to investigate things that appear to be unscientific. If a scientist was really looking for the truth God would show it to him,[49] but if he was looking for justification for his own arguments, that is what he would find.

On page 262 Dawkins is telling his readers that there is consensus about right and wrong that prevails surprisingly widely and that it has no obvious connection with religion. "Most people pay lip service to the same broad liberal consensus of ethical principles." I do not see that the principles recognized by Dawkins are very different from the four principles that were given to me at the beginning of my

---

message to the Gentiles. His letters to communities he had visited became books of the New Testament

[49] Consider the story of Madame Curie and radium. The discovery of penicillin.

journey by the force that I call God. I think Dawkins just needs to be introduced to God.

Page 221 – Dawkins proposes that the natural urge to be kind is like a natural sexual urge – it exists independently of what it was designed for. He says our moral sense like our sexual desire, is rooted deep in our Darwinian past. He says being kind is a Darwinian mistake but good. My comment was that being kind is a product of the force for good and Dawkins is trying to find a convoluted explanation for it because he knows that being kind does not fit in with the survival of the fittest that is the basis of evolutionary theory.

Page 223 – Dawkins refers to Hauser and his psychological experiments[50] - he says that in psychological experiments most people come to the same conclusion on moral issues even though they can't explain their reasons, and this shows that –

"driving our moral judgments, is a universal moral grammar, a faculty of the mind that evolved over millions of years to include a set of principles for building a range of possible moral systems. As with language, the principles that make up our moral grammar fly beneath the radar of our awareness - largely independent of religious beliefs or lack of them."

Unfortunately he doesn't specify the principles, but at least he accepts that there are principles, and that something is driving them, though he tries to find a complicated human explanation for this, while I would just say that the things of God are simple. We have

---

[50] Hauser – *Moral minds : How nature designed our universal sense of right and wrong.*

these principles because they are the product of the natural force for good – God to me – and that force communicates them to us and reminds us of them, by putting thoughts into our heads. Evil also makes suggestions to us and then we choose. If such a faculty of the mind had really evolved we would always choose the good.

Also on pages 223-4 he quotes some of Hauser's moral dilemmas. These are of the kind I would not use with children. For instance should we sacrifice one person to save five? But in the end they arrive at Kant's principle of not using people for our own ends – a maxim I have included in the principle of love. Dawkins claims that Kant says that this is a moral absolute, but quotes Hauser as saying that it is built into us by our evolution.

In communicating with the masses, simplicity wins over complicated theory every time. We are very unlikely to have to decide whether we should push a fat man off a bridge in order to save five others trapped on a railway line, but we are continually facing the situation of using others for our own ends. Every time we "pass the buck" instead of accepting responsibility that is rightfully ours, we are using other people for our own ends – to save ourselves some trouble. If we are kind to someone simply for what we can get from them in return, we are using them for our own ends. The God I know does not accept any individual just as collateral damage, but some people do choose to sacrifice themselves for others. That is usually motivated by love, but also, in some people at Kohlberg's highest level, by their own ethical principles.[51]

---

[51] After world War 2, Kohlberg studied why some people would put themselves in danger by helping others and produced his theory of moral reasoning

On page 269 Dawkins seems to be trying to show that humankind is improving ethically as Huxley and Darwin thought it might, and of course we are in some ways. We are not so openly racist or chauvinistic, but people like Judge Judy[52] say that criminals are getting younger. Crime is getting worse and I think our attitude to telling the truth is getting more lax. The level of white collar crime - and now internet crime - shows that a high I.Q. and a good education does not necessarily result in a high level of ethical reasoning. I am not quite sure if Dawkins is against all religions or if it is only the Christian God on whom he is concentrating his argument. On page 271 he says that Martin Luther King was a Christian, but that King had been influenced by Gandhi who was not a Christian. True, but Gandhi was not an atheist either. In the book "Pathway to God,"[53] it is stated that Gandhi thought of the whole of life as a pathway to God.

Quoting Ghandi himself, (ibid p5) - "God is certainly one. He has no second. He is unfathomable, unknowable and unknown to the vast majority of mankind. He is everywhere. He sees without eyes and hears without ears. He is formless and indivisible. He is uncreate, has no father, mother or child and yet He allows Himself to be worshipped as father, mother, wife and child.. He allows Himself even to be worshipped as stock and stone although He is none of those things. He is the most elusive. He is the nearest to us if we would but know the fact. But He is farthest from us when we do not want to realise his omnipresence. I dispute the description that Hindus are idolaters. They do say that there are many Gods, but they also declare

---

[52] Judy Scheindlin – An American Family Court Judge noted for T.V. and book, "Don't pee on my leg and tell me it's raining."(1997) Harper Collins

[53] Extracts from Gandhi's writings and speeches.(1971) compiled by M.S. Deshpande,. Navajivan Publishing House, Ahmendabad – 380 014

unmistakably that there is one God, the God of Gods." Through this passage alone we can see that Gandhi believed in a universal God - but not particularly the Christian God of the Trinity.

In spite of his claim that God is a delusion, on page 272, Dawkins almost verifies my belief in God as the force for good in the world. He says, "It is probably not a single force like gravity, but a complex interplay of disparate forces like the one that propels Moore's law describing the exponential increase in computer power." He says, "Whatever its cause, the manifest phenomenon of Zeitgeist[54] progression is more than enough to undermine the claim that we need God in order to be good, or to decide what is good." I give my thanks to Dawkins. At least he accepts that there is a cause.

Finally, I was particularly interested in his chapter in defense of children.. There is so much with which I agree, especially that to choose wisely, one must be in full possession of the facts. Certainly children should learn in school about other religions and what they believe, but it is not only religions that indoctrinate children. This is a point where I feel Dawkins is light on justice. He spends several pages on the faults of the Amish communities, but only a passing reference to cruel initiation ceremonies of other cultures. Fundamentalist religions indoctrinate children. Mainline religions indoctrinate children. Communism and Nazism indoctrinated children. Most parents indoctrinate their children by speech or example. Society indoctrinates children by the type of material they are exposed to inside and outside their homes. I agree with Dawkins about post-modernists and relativists (pp 328-9) and the conflict involved

---

[54] Zeitgeist (German) – the general outlook of a specific time or period.

in maintaining cultural diversity. We can respect the cultures of different ethnic groups and treat the people themselves with respect, but when it comes to making ethical decisions in a multi-cultural society, relativism fails. The ethical principles that God gave me at the beginning of my voyage were given as a Global ethic to provide a simple solution to that problem today.

There is danger in convincing ourselves that there is a "Zeitgeist" progression upwards towards the good, We may become careless about ways in which the progression is also downwards. Evil is there waiting. Destroying faith in God will not produce a perfect society. Communism proved that. Suppressing religion did not produce a better society. Greed, envy and selfishness still found fertile ground. In our search for the truth, we need to keep all four principles in mind. If he keeps searching for the truth maybe Dawkins will recognize God one day, and then write another book affirming a force for good. One big flash of knowledge to open his eyes and he could be working for the other side. He could be the Saint Paul of the future, turning from persecuting the religious of his day, to becoming a leader in a new religion based on a new knowledge of a force for good.

3.3.13

Yesterday, in the week-end newspaper[55] there was an article telling how, by implanting electrodes in the brains of two rats, scientists now claimed to have proved that information can be transferred by brain waves. These electrodes were one hundredth the width of a human hair but when the "encoded" rat pressed a lever an electrical version of its brain activity was transferred to the "receiver" rat in another

---

[55] Collins, N.(2013, March 2) Mind-reading a step closer. N.Z. Herald p B 7.

cage thousands of miles away, and 70% of the time the receiver rat performed the same action. Scientists consider 70% to be well above the level of chance – and of course 100% of the messages might have got through, but like us, a considerable proportion of the time the receiver might have chosen to ignore them.

22

GOOD INTENTIONS

At the end of the Chapter on Reason, I said that it was understandable that the Institutions that grew up around the messages of the prophets believed they must keep the message pure and that they had had the best of intentions. The best of intentions however don't always ensure that we are on the right paths, or that they will have the consequences we planned..

On the 18th December 2009 I wrote -

"The vicar of a large city church in ------ has erected a bill-board with a sexual theme of Joseph and Mary in bed together - and with Joseph worried that he had a hard act to follow. The reason claimed for the billboard was that it was intended to promote discussion about the validity of the Christmas story. I wonder if the subject was brought up during the discussions in 2007-8. It would be good to know that there actually was debate on this subject, and it is encouraging for me to see the question brought out into the open by those within the church. When I began this journey, I was so frightened that I was going to have to go alone into a lion's den, even if God was going to be with me.

It had taken courage to bring up the subject, but unfortunately the emphasis had been put on sex in such a way that the bill-board was offensive to many rather than encouraging debate about the subject, especially at Christmas time, and that is how it will probably be remembered. Another example of how evil takes every opportunity to distort the things of God. I remember from my young days, a saying that was common then, 'The road to hell is paved with good intentions.' If I'd thought about the meaning then, I would have assumed that it meant something like 'Good intentions are not always enough to produce good results.' I can see now that even though our intentions are good, evil can sometimes take them and use them in a harmful way."

The vicar of the church explained that from the Church's teaching, people saw God in human form, but he wanted people to see God as a force of love. However, I do not see in today's world that sex really equates with love. Young people are very influenced by what they see on Television or in films. That is real life to them, and what they see usually tells them that a night out and some physical attraction should automatically end up with a night in bed - and there is always the morning-after pill. I see little love in people indulging in one night stands, or in drunken teen-agers having sex with people they hardly know – or in people using others for their own ends. Sex is part of the animal instinct to reproduce. There is a lot more to love than sex, and that is where the good intentions went wrong. Paul's description of love in First Corinthians Chapter 13[56] would have been a far more

---

[56] See page 103

accurate picture of God as the force of love, but of course it would have attracted far less attention.

I do not think that any human can completely explain God, who is infinite and beyond complete human understanding., but how else can we talk about God except in the words we know. It is not a case of God being either this or that, and limiting God to what our human intellects can devise. One of the things God showed me is that He can be all things to all people, whatever their needs may be. The God I know is much more than the force of love.

When I think about it, I realise that I do not see God in human form, and yet I know Him as a friend and someone I can talk to.

I know Him as the force for good in the world.

I know His power as the power of love, but I also know Him as an identity that personally cares about every individual human being

I have also experienced Him as a presence - awe-inspiring in a way that I could never have imagined, and yet as I wrote in the beginning, infinite love, infinite power and also infinite capacity for suffering as He personally feels the suffering of His people here on earth.

He is also a God of justice who is waiting and hoping to keep His side of the covenant made so long ago, but who will not interfere if humans decide to choose a path that will lead to their own destruction.

23

AND NOW THE MESSAGES

It was in the dictation of the messages that I have experienced God most forcefully as a presence – an awe-inspiring power that surrounded me, communicated with me, and then released me when I had done what I had been required to do. But why would anyone believe what I write here? I can only say, "Look at my past history. Have I ever written fantasy? Have I ever shown that I have a vivid imagination? I am a farmer. I am a practical person. I write about what I know and what I have experienced. I do not spend time trying to be a clever writer - trying to impress other writers and my readers with imaginative metaphors and extensive descriptions. I write as I would speak to my friends and I tell my story as it was. I am still having difficulty trying to find the right words to describe the atmosphere when I wrote these messages, so I can understand that readers will have difficulty in believing that I am telling the truth.

I was told that if the church would not listen to me, I was to go to the people and time is running out. If the church won't accept the message, then as long as I get it into print, others may believe me, and at least some of the people will accept that God has sent it.

These messages came in the night – much more powerful than any of the messages I was shown in parables or in flashes of knowledge. They were dictated to me, and I was given what I was to write, phrase by phrase or word by word. The force or identity that was dictating them would not continue until I had written what I had been given, and even after I had been released I was too overwhelmed to move for several minutes.

Copy of the message as written in my pad used at night in 1976.

"I command you all as you shall answer at the dreadful day of judgment, to give me my share of the covenant which was made with you on the first day of Pentecost so long ago. The first fruits of your crop of fine young men and women to be a Holy and living sacrifice to the end that those who believe in Me shall not perish, but have everlasting life. Amen.

The second message that came in 1977 was more frightening.

"I command you all as you shall answer at the dreadful day of judgment to give me my share of the first fruits of your crop of fine young men and women.

Verily, verily, I say unto you that unless you give me my share of the covenant which was made with you on the first day of Pentecost so long ago, the world will be taken over by the powers of darkness and Christianity will vanish from the face of the earth."

I have written on this page – "Copy of the message that was dictated with such power. Not God as my friend, but God the awe-inspiring – the ultimate authority."

My knowledge of God as the force for good and a loving father, assures me that the day of judgment will not be a wrathful God coming to destroy the people He made. Nor will He separate out "Christians" and give them a beautiful world to live in on their own.- or any other sect or branch of religion. We are all in this together and the day of judgment will come to us all if we pollute the earth beyond recovery. We will have brought it on ourselves and Christians will not be exempt. They have been warned.

The first fruit of the crop to be given to God will be those who will have the courage to question the traditional teachings of the Christian church and offer the masses an alternative. They will offer a version of Christianity that the educated masses of today can accept. They will teach the truth about Jesus, and when he is lifted up as an ordinary man, not a god, but an ordinary man filled with the Holy Spirit, he will really draw all men to him. He will be the inspiration and example of the heights to which ordinary people may go to prevent the world from being taken over by the powers of darkness. (And surely we can see those powers of darkness already in action in this new movement in the Middle East and the atrocities they seem to take a delight in committing. Just visualizing the caging and burning of a Jordanian pilot reminds me of the flashes of absolute malevolence I have been allowed to see in the past. If they have been convinced that they are doing such things for their god, that is an example of evil pretending to be God.)

The sacrifice that Christians will make will remove the main barrier between the "people of the book," Jews, Christians and Muslims - and perhaps will be the bridge that will allow progress to be made. But God is a God of justice, and God has no favourites. If Christians are going to make a sacrifice, Judaism and Islam will have sacrifices of their own to make, they will have their own messengers, but Christians will have to take the first step.

Martin Luther had the courage to question the established church of his day. It is not impossible and the conditions could be right.

In an undated writing from the old folder I found –

"Nobody should envy those who lead. It will take exceptional men, and their burdens would be overwhelming to lesser mortals. They will need exceptional women as their partners to inspire and encourage them. In their own life-time they may not feel that they have achieved a great deal, but to put a wheel into reverse will take far more effort than will ever be required once it is moving the right way -- but their personal reward will be great."

We were also given instructions on what to do and where to start.

"We are to start with the children and be patient. It is too late for this generation of children, but we are to provide the teachers washed with the Holy Spirit, and the Holy Spirit will see that the children come to be taught."

Another message on the same page – "When you're cleaning a room, you start at the top and work down." (To me this referred to the leaders of the Church.)

Reading this page over in 1996 I had written – "I must point out that the children are not necessarily young children, but can mean new Christians who are being brought into the Church."

Now in 2015, nearly twenty years on from 1996, and nearly forty years on from the time they were dictated, I can see that though those messages were dictated for the Christian world, the Christian Church was also being told that it needed to enlist the help of the masses. People do not need to be members of a Christian Church to help in the fight against evil - against the powers of darkness – and they need to help for the sake of the generations to come.

****

24

HOPE

P art of the task I was given was to offer hope to a despairing people. It is difficult to view the situation in the Middle East today without an element of despair. How can this tide of the power of evil be reversed without resorting to greater violence? We need hope if we are to make the effort that it will take to find an answer, but if we believe we are on our own with only our own resources to rely on, it would be easy to despair and say, "The whole situation is hopeless. Let them kill each other off. Why not live for ourselves and live for today?" But this would only hasten the end of humans as a species. The human species is on a downward slope, but the chain reaction should not be allowed to go any further. Someone needs to accept the load caused by the mistakes of the past. "Passing the buck" is the easy option when we are faced with a difficult decision, but it will not do now. If a new generation is prepared to shoulder the burden caused by the mistakes of previous generations, they will be amazed how light that burden will turn out to be - and how great the rewards.

We should not underestimate the power that could be released to help us, once we make the choice to try. All through my journey over the last forty years, I have found that God waits until I have made an effort myself, and then He will help and make the seemingly impossible task possible, and easier than I thought. Evil tries to persuade you that the task is too hard and you are completely inadequate, so why not just take the easy way out and live for today - but God asks us to look at the long-term consequences of our actions – or inaction - and their effect on other people. These other people will be our own descendents. All of our grandchildren were here for my 88th Christmas, and as I looked at these fine young people I wondered how many of us would gather together the next Christmas, and where their lives would take them. Would they be the generation that turns the world around? Would it be the next generation – my great grand-children? The first leaves are falling from the trees. We do not have much time left to make our choice. We need to make the effort while we can still see the sun.

If the God I know isn't seen so clearly in organized religion by ordinary people today, it is not God's fault. He is still there waiting for the masses and wanting them to see Him as He really is. He still cares for them and sends other people to help them, even though those people may not realize that it is God who sends them. Evil is clever but not wise. In the end, it gets carried away by pride in its own cleverness and goes too far. God gave us free will and we make our own choices. Perhaps God has needed to allow evil to take over to the extent that people would see for themselves how a world without God (the force for good) would be. How can humans treat each other in the way the victims of civil wars are being treated today? Look at the faces of the children and other refugees. I can see the utter malevolence of the force of evil behind the decisions that opposing factions are making – suggesting to the leaders, "What do these ordinary people matter? Hold on. You will win. You will have the power in the end."

Only when the human race has truly had enough of evil, when people truly want to do better and start to fight back, will the real God, the force for good in the world, pour out the power that will be available to help them overcome the evil that is often pretending to be their God. People have to choose for themselves, and want to make a better world. God wants us to choose the good. He has always wanted people to choose good. Written records as far back as Moses in the Old Testament speak of His Covenant with the people. "Today I am giving you a choice between good and evil, between life and death. Choose life."[57] It is not necessary for the masses to go to Church on Sunday, or be a part of organized religion to know God, but mankind needs the record of God's dealing with people of all cultures that organized religion maintains. There will always be a need for organized religion in order to keep this record - an unending scroll. But organized religion puts full-stops where there should only be commas. God is not dead. God is not a delusion. God is waiting for the time to be right – and for the right people to emerge as leaders.

I was given two tasks to do. The first was to put the ethical teaching I had received from God into a form that could be accepted by ordinary people in the multicultural societies we have now become. I would be providing a "Global Ethic" which would apply

---

[57] Deuteronomy Ch 30 v 15 -19 See, I have set before you today, life and good. death and evil --- ----choose life. (ESV)

to the values of all races and cultures. I have done that. I have put it on the internet where it is freely available to anyone who is interested, but I have yet to discover what more I can do. When people had accepted an ethic that was not based on religion, but on reason, then I was to write about the source of my information. I had to write about the God - the force for good I know, so that I could introduce Him to the wandering flock. I had learned that the masses of people will not bother with anything that is too confusing, or is in a language that they don't understand. I had to make it short and simple. Have I done that?

- God is the force for good in this world, but there is also an active force for evil that is more tempting with its short-term rewards. Both forces communicate with us by putting thoughts into our heads. We have free will and we make our own choices. Today mankind must make its choice. The first leaves are falling from the trees. We can choose which way we go. Uphill into the sunshine is the harder way, but the alternative is to slide downwards into the darkness. That should be plain enough for anyone. The task may seem impossible but we have hope. If we choose the harder way God will help us, but we will need no help to slide downwards. – And evil will be gloating – and giving us a push.

- There is truth in the Bible, but it is not always historical or literal truth as we see it from our point in time. In the same way there is truth in the sacred writings of other religions.

We can understand the Bible much better if we look at the characters and the writers of the various books as real people of their times. They interpreted events against the background of their times and within the limits of their own knowledge. The traditions and customs of in the main, less educated people, have shaped all our religions. Today, with the knowledge we have at our disposal, we should be able to look at all the faiths and examine them for the truth. If we strip away the trimmings that have been added, and return to the messages of their prophets, accepting that they spoke with the knowledge they had at that time, we should be on firm ground and have hope for the future. The spirit that speaks through the good in all religions is surely the same spirit that has guided mankind upwards since evolution began.

* * * * * * * * *

25

INTO THE FUTURE

W hen I began this journey in the 1970s, the baby boomers – the children who were born in the years just after World War 2 ended, and when my generation had resumed as normal a life as possible – were young adults. There were also adults who had been young children during the war. They were now reacting to the war in Vietnam and its consequences. Many were high on ideals or deep in disillusion.

Here are some extracts from my notes in my oldest file

I wrote most of this section back in the late 1970s, and I doubt if my style of writing then would be considered acceptable to-day. (Sexist language too)

* * * * * * * * * *

"Angry young men and women of the 60s and 70s marched in processions and demonstrated on pavements about the establishment, its restrictions, its hypocrisy and its wicked ways. They talked about love and smelled the flowers. They asked the questions then, but it seems that they did not find the right answers. Evil distracted them with its attractive short-term answers. Take the easy way. Drugs make you feel good. Do your own thing. Love is all you need – and those who survived that period became the leaders, politicians, law-makers and trend-setters of the next thirty years. We became a consumer society, consuming and wasting at a rate never before seen, indulging ourselves in every way. Individualism and "rights" became the fastest growing ethical trends over the last half of the twentieth century. New generations may be able to survey the last hundred years, and, with the advantages of hind-sight, see where the mistakes have been made. Were the right questions asked? Were the right trends followed?

We still have time, but only just. The bugle calls today for those who are prepared to listen, for those who are young and have visions of the future, for mothers and fathers who care about their children and the grandchildren to come. There is work for all to do. Good work, challenging work, demanding work, exhausting work, work for a goal that will be well worth the effort. Nothing worth having comes easily in this world, and the force of evil will fight us all the way. The rewards will be great. There will be self-respect and dignity. There will be the gratitude of the generations to come who will say thanks for protecting their world and not letting them down. Thanks for stopping the slide in time, and moving into reverse so that they too can have their share of all the good things we have had in abundance."

"Young people need a cause and they are good at heart.

They need to fight and we need to give them something worth-while to fight for.

They admire courage and we must show them courage.

They have a right to live life to the full.

They have a right to know about the good things that life has to offer so they can make reasoned choices.

Why should they settle for less?

If we lower our standards every time the going gets a bit tough, in the end we go backwards.

If we alter the rules of the game because it is difficult to keep to them, the prize will become less valuable and in the end there will be no prize at all.

Our descendents have a right to their share of the resources we are squandering today – to open spaces, clean rivers, green forests and fresh air.

They have a right to see the stars, sparkling and flashing in the clear night air.

They have a right to see the tops of mountains and far-off hills without a murky film between.

They have a right to experience true love and the joys and sorrows of real family life. Yes - sorrows too, because without the sorrows they will never quite know the glory of the heights.

They have a right to a challenge and a goal and all the struggles that bring out the best in a human being.

But they need a map and guidelines so that they will not waste time running this way and that with no hope of reaching their goal.

The mistakes of the past may never be erased from the book of history, but they have the opportunity now to write history for themselves and those who follow them. This generation could be remembered as the people who marked the turning point in mankind's existence on earth - the point in time when the advantages of science, history, global travel and communication came together to provide the opportunity that had never existed before. They have their choice while they can still see the sun."

"The Christian 'New Jerusalem,' the 'Kingdom of God on earth' is something that people themselves of all races and religions – or no religions - can work towards. It should be the goal in all our personal and political thinking. It will be mankind's best achievement, our finest hour, and it will be reached with the help of the spirit of God who will enter more and more into the hearts of people who want a better world. The 'Kingdom of God' will be here on earth when people of different races and cultures live together as one family because they want to. They will know they are family because they all have the same Father God – whatever they may call the force for good. They could live forever in a beautiful world that they will protect because they will honour it as their mother. This is the goal, and it is within mankind's power to reach it. This is no time for despair, but it is a time for action and a combined fight against evil. We are all part of God's overall plan, and if the part we have to play is that of soldiers, a fighting people who will stand against evil, then what more exciting prospect could mankind have in store? What more worthy cause for young people, than to fight for all the principles of God – wisdom, justice, truth and love, against the offerings of evil, greed, selfishness, hatred and injustice? Fine 'upright' young men and women could be inspired to fight for good in the sure knowledge that though they may only carry the baton part of the way, their side is going to win in the end."

"The message and the man in the street.

We must enlist the help of the 'man in the street,' encourage him, involve him and speak to him in terms he can understand about problems to which he can relate. If the people cannot believe there is a God, they can at least equate God with good and be enlisted to fight against evil. God's timing is always perfect. While the Christian waits and wonders if God has forgotten His promises, evil takes over to the point where the masses themselves are looking for help. We must enlist their help in the fight against evil."

* * * * * * * * * *

Nearly forty years on, and the force pretending to be God has had a successful time in antagonizing a good section of the masses against Christianity – to the point in this country at least, where a government has considered we are no longer a Christian country. Much of my writing in the 1970s was concerned with warning the charismatic church about turning in on itself, being too exclusive and alienating the "second-class" Christians. Also warning church leaders to teach the truth. I had been told I was to act as a liaison between the Church and the masses. It is going to be much harder now. I wrote then that we could say to the masses, "Even if you do not believe in the spiritual side of Christianity, can you accept the Christian principles as laid down by Jesus Christ as being a sound basis for a better world?" The answer today in many quarters would probably be "No. We want nothing that has anything to do with religion – especially Christianity."

I know how evil is influencing thought against the Christian religion, but I also see how, by pretending to be God, evil is influencing the Christian religion to hasten its own demise where the masses are concerned. Different groups provide the evidence that is used to claim that God is only a delusion – that humans created God. And yet I know that God's timing is right. I have to use the right language, and explain the God I know in terms to which they can relate. New wine in new bottles for a modern world. The same message, but put in a way that can be accepted.

The sacrifice that Christians are going to have to make in the end is to admit their mistakes. I can see the influence of evil pretending to be God and persuading them to cling to their dogma, honestly believing they are keeping the faith. Progress can only be made though, if the teachers have the courage to speak the truth.[58]

Evil tells me I have made a mistake somewhere and of course is having a great time trying to make me feel confused and guilty, but it is not succeeding. It affects my pride because I don't want to make mistakes, but I don't let it panic me because I know that whatever it is, God will be able to take it and use it for a victory over evil. My work over recent years has included battling the local District Council over their Rural Plan Change, battling the Ministry of Education and politicians over values education in their proposed curriculum, trying to finish my resource material, getting my web-site set up and at the same time, trying to live the normal life of a normal person of my age – and to appear normal to all those around me. I have trouble sleeping but no wonder my brain is so active that it won't let go at night. Maybe my mistake has been to say that evil cannot do anything physical. This morning my computer seems to have had a mind of its own and it has taken me several hours to do a task that should have only taken one.

---

[58] Another reminder today though (4.6.'07). Don't drive them into a dead end with no exit. Allow them a way out with dignity.

In judging me, don't forget that nobody is perfect. As God said to me in the beginning, "Don't always be looking for signs and symbols. I have given you wisdom. Use it in my service." That was not just meant for me. God has given us brains and expects us to use them. It is one thing making a mistake accidentally. That can be attended to as soon as you realize it, but it is quite another thing to deliberately cling to a mistake and its consequences, simply because you don't want to admit you were wrong. I don't really like admitting my mistakes to other people, but the Church itself says that PRIDE is the cardinal sin. If Christianity has made mistakes over the last two thousand years, other religions have also made mistakes. It shouldn't be too difficult in this modern world to recognize the mistakes and try to correct them and do better in future, but PRIDE is going to be a stumbling block for all of us.

"Carpe diem" – seize today. That quotation has become very popular in recent years. It continues - "And put as little trust as you can in tomorrow," The quotation can be used to justify self-indulgence or it can be used to inspire us to make the most of every day – to do as much good as we can because even if we are not here tomorrow, other people and our descendants will have to live with the consequences of what we do today.

26

CONCLUSION

I have been working on this book for several years now. I have to satisfy myself that it is the best I can do. Each time I go through it I can see some correction, improvement or addition I should make. I write messages to myself, but I can take no chances now - time may be running out for me, so I must conclude, and endeavour to get my information somehow into the public domain. Maybe the only people who will read what I have written will be people who want to make a difference – but that could be enough. I was told I would be sowing seeds, but I have no idea where they will grow. I was also told that we would light a fire that will sweep the world. As we have seen over this dry summer of 2014-15, one tiny spark can light a fire that with the right wind, will sweep over a huge area. Sometimes, but rarely now, there is another parable to be seen or message to be heard or emphasized.

June 2011 –Note to myself. Make sure you end by giving them hope. Remember God said that when they decide to make an effort they will not be alone. He will help, and what at first might seem to be an impossible task and so it is not worth trying, will become possible. But it is up to people themselves. They will have to want to make a difference.

July 2011 – Those who went before us have not been wrong about the force they called Satan. There *is* a force for evil. It tries to influence our thinking. It breathes hatred and dissension and does everything it can to help us destroy ourselves and this world.

Writing in 2012 - The problem for the Christian Church as I see it is that those who have the courage to speak out in the search for truth will have to cope with the force of evil pretending to be God, and influencing the minds of others who genuinely believe they are on God's side. I can merely repeat the message I was given – that one building must not be destroyed until another one has been built alongside it. The branches must not fight against each other. Give the people a choice and leave the result to God.

10.3 2013 – I was doing one of the readings in church this morning – the parable of the prodigal son. I had always had a lot of sympathy with the elder son who had worked faithfully for his father, while the other son had gone off to spend his inheritance. I could understand how the elder son must have felt when his brother was welcomed home so lavishly, but in the middle of the reading I had another of those flashes of knowledge. - That is how the established church will feel if a younger brother grows up beside it and appears to be favoured by the father. I nearly lost my place in the reading, but knew I had to tell the established church how much the father appreciates its work and faithfulness over the last two thousand years.

Don't resent the younger brother. You will need each other in the future. God is a God of justice as well as a God of love.

I have never wanted to upset the Christian Church. Some of the people who belong to fundamentalist Christian churches are among the kindest and most sincere people I know. I can only hope that they will not be too upset by what I have been compelled to write. I have to complete the task I was given. I hope they will understand that. If the Church of today is not interested in hearing the message, I have to go to the wandering flock. I have to offer an alternative belief for those who cannot accept the dogma of the Christian Church and all its creeds - an alternative that the educated masses of today may be able to accept. I have explained a great deal about the God I came to know through my experiences over the last forty years or more, though the masses may find it difficult to believe what I have experienced. I can only repeat that the God I know insists on truth, justice and concern for all people. He is a God of reason who expects us to consider the consequences of our actions. What I write is the truth as I know it now. It may not be all of the truth that there is to know. I have never known God to act against what we see as the laws of nature, but we do not yet know all there is to know about those laws. Humans cannot dare to put a limit on God, because there is a limit to human understanding. It is arrogant of humans to limit God to what they can understand.

Father God is spirit, loving, just, caring about each individual, encouraging us as a species to take the difficult steps, and there to help us if we fall. He created humans in His own image, spiritual or physical, to commune with Him and to look after the environment

He had provided for us. Each individual human being possesses some of His spirit while they live.

Hinduism believes that the human soul or spirit is like a drop of water emerging as spray from an ocean, and at death merging back into the ocean again, while Christians are told to believe in the resurrection of the body, and an individual soul that exists beyond death. I write about what I have experienced so far and death is yet to come. It will be another interesting experience.

Looking through my earlier writings recently, I found one that read, -

"I had never been sure about a life hereafter. I had thought maybe heaven was here on earth for those who loved God and tried to obey him. Now I knew, once and for all that there is a life with God after death, that my parents were already there and knew that I honoured them."

Perhaps I will have a choice. Perhaps I will just stay a while, and some of the spirit I have been given will return in another human form. God's ways are broad enough to accommodate all mankind. Even if this book gets published and the wandering masses accept what I have to say, I think that I will not be here to see it. My husband died recently after nearly sixty-four years together. Will we meet again in an afterlife? Will he be there waiting to greet me? I really don't know, but I had a dream a few years ago, and can I end my story in any better way than with this piece that I wrote in 2008 -

April 2008

I am writing this here in case I lose the bit of paper I wrote it on in the middle of the night recently.

I had been having difficulty sleeping as is usual when my brain is active, and had put on a C.D. I have always loved waltz time and was thinking as I listened that waltz time is really in tune with nature. 2-4 is abrupt and marching time, but 3-4 is smooth like the swinging of a pendulum or the seasons in nature. Nothing jerky, but something that just happens by itself as the energy runs out at the top, then starts to gain once more with the fall. I have never worried much about what happens after death, but as I was drifting off I saw myself at the end of this life – and I then had to get up and write it down - "waltzing away into a place of love with the souls of those whom I have loved and who have loved me." I was very tempted to just enjoy the feeling and drift into sleep without writing it down, but right from the beginning and all through this, I have known that I have to write down things as soon as I receive them because I may not remember in the morning. When I die, that is how I would like those I love to see me. My soul will be waiting to meet theirs in a place of love.

* * * * * * * *

PART 2

MESSAGES FROM DIARY 2

This seems to be the place to write a selection of the messages that were shown to me, or given to me as I learned about the work I was to do and the information I was to pass on. I had wondered whether I should include these in a book for the wandering flock, but then I remembered that I had been one of the wandering flock myself – just getting on with life with no particular wish to work for God. Probably there are people out there now, unaware of the plans God has for them. Maybe something I have written here will be used to inspire eyes to see and ears to hear.

For me, often these messages came as parables as I worked around the farm. Sometimes they were scraps of a conversation overheard, that jumped out at me and I had that flash of knowledge that was never my own thinking. Wherever I have added comments of my own to explain what was shown to me, I have put my own comments in brackets. Because they are parables, what they meant to me at the time may apply in the future to a different situation and mean something different to another person who has eyes to see and ears to hear. If there are things that we do not understand now, it may be because it is not the right time for us to understand. The right people may not be in place. When the conditions are right, God will show us. Though one message may not necessarily follow immediately on another, there are themes running through the messages, and these themes are simple.

There is an active force for good in the world, but also an active force for evil. We choose which one we will listen to.

The offerings of the force of evil are always more immediate, brighter and more attractive. Evil's ultimate goal is for humanity to destroy itself and its environment.

The offerings of the force for good are quieter, not so easy, but they are long lasting and work for the good of all mankind.

There is one God or force for good that has communicated with all religions showing them His ethical standards. Eventually all religions need to accept that God is the umbrella over all humanity.

The Christian religion will have to make the first move and it will need to sacrifice some of its traditional teaching.

A new branch of Christianity will need to be allowed to grow alongside the old and God will choose which one will survive.

A reader will see these themes as I learned them through messages or parables.

At first I was so bewildered by what was happening to me that I was constantly looking for directions and signs and signals. I was told –

"Don't be always looking for signs and signals. I have given you wisdom. Trust it and use it for me."

"Get on with the work I have given you to do here."

"Love is there like a perennial plant. Remove the weeds from the surface and love will come up."

"Build the new house up against the old, and leave the old one standing until the new one is ready."

"When we get a bit further along there will be a road and a bridge that we didn't know was there."

"Start out in the right direction and allow ourselves to be led by God."

"Extra clothes are there in the Bible to put on when it gets cold."

"The things of God are very simple. They follow the eternal principles and they work for the good of all people."

"When we are in a dangerous position, we must have something firm to which we can cling."

"We will have to leave our nice warm comfortable beds and go out in the cold."

"No sensible gardener would plant good seeds in ground that was covered with weeds. He would get rid of the weeds first."

"People need to be shown which are the good plants and which are the weeds."

"Love can remain dormant in the ground. As soon as the weeds are cleared it will come up."

"No good gardener is going to allow his crop to be completely smothered by weeds."

"The lesson is never more important than the people you are trying to teach. – People come first."

"When you reach out your hand to someone in trouble you reach out your hand to God."

"Firstly concern for the individual, then the wider concern for all people."

"God's will will be done in the end. It is only man's slowness that is holding us up."

"We need a continuing record of man's personal experience with God, otherwise theory becomes separated from reality and so loses credibility in the eyes of the people."

"It is far easier to keep a garden free of weeds than it is to get rid of them once they have taken over."

"Keep a wound covered if you want it to heal quickly."

"First there is God – the eternal Father – all things to all people for all time according to their needs."

"Evil would like to destroy us through the things that are important to us."

"Evil's favourite way of getting at you is through your love for your family."

"One of Evil's nasty little ways is to confuse us, getting us to run this way and that, to distract us from God's purpose for us"

"The cross must be set in a firm foundation otherwise it will not stand."

"God provides the opportunities, but we have to act on them."

"While we are talking the weeds are growing. Start with the children and be patient."

"No matter how eager you are to help, your efforts are wasted if you won't do as you are asked."

"The young will swallow anything if no-one teaches them what is good for them."

"The bridge will be near the old stump."

"Once we have made the bridge, we will be able to get at the weeds in the other pastures."

"Once we get over the bridge, we will be able to share the best that everyone else has to offer."

(I have understood the bridge as something that will enable us to connect with other religions – most likely a reform of Christianity)

"You may search the world looking for more light, but you won't find it unless you do what God has asked you to do at home."

"If we don't feed them properly, they will lose the weight they have gained."

"They need a varied diet or they will get digestive disorders."

"If you don't do the work properly it will be taken from you and given to others."

"The second crop will be the best." (Christianity.)

"God has provided us with enough food in good times to see us through the bad."

"God will give us enough power to get up the hill."

"While there is a drought we can get into places we would never have been able to reach otherwise."

"The new baby may be a nuisance but we are responsible for him." (The new baby to me is the new branch of the Christian Church.)

"Once they see the green grass, they'll come running for it." (To me, the green grass is the new teaching.)

"Evil is at work all the time distracting our attention, trying to make us forget the message Jesus brought. Keep it beside you all the time, "Turn from evil and turn to good and the Kingdom of God is at hand."

"When you need some advice, go to the expert."

"If we don't get things under control now, it will be a long cold winter. Evil keeps telling us we can start tomorrow. We must make a start today."

"She nearly lost her baby once. She will be very anxious not to lose him again."

"There will be no permanent cure in treating symptoms. We must get at the cause, but things have to get sufficiently bad for us to be able to find the cause."

"We must provide the service our master expects for his customers. First ask what he would have done in those circumstances."

"How He must suffer to see the light go out of their eyes."

"If people call and get no reply, they will go elsewhere. We must be able to respect our leaders."

* * * * * * * * * *

EPILOGUE

In the epilogue to her highly academically researched book, *"The case for God: What religion really means,"* (2009,) Karen Armstrong states-

> *"Socratic dialogue was never aggressive;*
> *rather it was conducted with courtesy,*
> *gentleness and consideration. If a dialogue*
> *aroused malice or spite, it would fail.*
> *There was no question of forcing your*
> *interlocutor to accept your point of view:*
> *Instead each offered his opinion as a gift to*
> *the others; allowed them to alter their*
> *own perceptions .....*
> *Socrates, Plato and Aristotle, the founders of Western rationalism,*
> *saw no opposition between reason and the transcendent"*

In this same spirit my story is offered as a gift to the ongoing discussion as to whether God is dead, a delusion, or still exists as an active force for good that science has not identified yet: a force that cares about humanity - offers ideas, but allows us the freedom to make our own choices, and take the consequences - for good or evil.

REFERENCES

Scripture quotations are mainly from the The Holy Bible, English Standard Version, Copyright @ 2001 by Crossway Bibles a division of Good News Publishers. Printed for the Bible Societies. The copyright information printed in the first pages of this edition states that the ESV text may be quoted in written form - up to one thousand verses - without written permission of the publisher, providing that the verses quoted do not amount to more than 50% of the total text of the work in which they are quoted.

The Living Bible - Paraphrased (copyright 1971) 21st printing, May 1973. USA. Tyndale House Publishers, Wheaton, Illinois 60187 ISBN 8423-2250-7

The Baha'is. (1994 edition) Published by the Baha'i Publishing Trust of the United Kingdom. Leistershire, U.K. Printed in the USA. ISBN 1-870989-37-6

Allegro, J. (1964) *The Dead Sea Scrolls: A Reappraisal.*(2nd ed.) Great Britain: Penguin Books

Armstrong, K. (2009 The Bodley Head). *The Case for God: What religion means.*(This Large print edition 2010) by BBC Audiobooks Ltd by arrangement with the Random House Group Ltd. U.K. Windsor/Paragon

Barrett, D., *"Annual statistic table on Global Mission 1997."* Cited in Noll 1997. Blaiklock, E.M. (1977). *Commentary on the New Testament.* P54. U.K.: Hodder and Stoughton.

Collins, N.(2013, March 2) Mind-reading a step closer. N.Z. Herald p B 7.

Dawkins, R. (2006). *The God Delusion.* London:Transworld publishers.

Gandhi, M. (1980). *The spirit of Hinduism.* New Delhi: Pankaj Publications.

Gandhi, M. (1971). *Pathway to God.* Ahmedabad: Navajivan Publishing House.

Green, V., (1996). Chapter 11: 'The Crisis of the modern Church' (p351) in *A new history of Christianity.*

Hauser – *Moral minds : How nature designed our universal sense of right and wrong.* Cited in Dawkins, (2006) p222

Hinman, L. (1998). *Ethics: A pluralistic approach to moral theory.* (2nd ed.). San Diego: Harcourt Brace

Jung Chang, (2005) *Mao: The unknown Story.* Jonathan Cape.

Keown, P. (2001) Weak, indecisive and ineffectual? Towards a national dialogue in values education through social studies. *Delta* 53, (1&2), pp43-60

Keown, P. (2005). *Report on values in the N.Z. Curriculum.*

Kohlberg, L. (1976). The cognitive-developmental approach to moral education. Ch 12 in Purpel & Ryan (Eds.) *Moral education: It comes with the territory.* USA: McCutchan (pp176-195)

McGlone, M. (1983) *Scientific Creationism. The Bible says No,* (unpublished?) Auckland University New Zealand

Noll, M. (1997) 2nd ed. 2000. *Turning points: Decisive moments in the history of Christianity.* USA : Baker Academic.

Noss, D. and Noss, J. (1994) *A history of the world's religions.* (9th ed.) USA :

Macmillan College Publishing Co.

Purpel and Ryan (1976) *Moral education: It comes with the territory.* USA McCutchan.

Sheindlin, J. (1996) *Don't pee on my leg and tell me it's raining.* USA: Harper Perennial.

Smart. N., (1971) The religious experience of mankind. (3rd ed.) UK: Collins. P 664

Wilson. J.A. (1977 edition) Egypt : The Values of Life. Chapters III & IV in H and H. Frankfort, W. Irwin, T. Jacobsen and J. Wilson (Eds) *The intellectual adventure of ancient man,* (pp89-100) USA: University of Chicago Press

1ST CORINTHIANS
CHAPTER 13 VS.1-13. (ESV)

"If I speak in the tongues of men and of angels, but have not love, I am a noisy gong or a clanging cymbal. And if I have prophetic powers, and understand all mysteries and all knowledge, and if I have all faith so as to move mountains, but have not love, I am nothing. If I give away all I have, and if I deliver up my body to be burned, but have not love, I gain nothing.

Love is patient and kind; love does not envy or boast; it is not arrogant or rude. It does not insist on its own way; it is not irritable or resentful; it does not rejoice at wrong-doing but rejoices with the truth. Love bears all things, believes all things, hopes all things, endures all things.

Love never ends. As for prophecies, they will pass away; as for tongues they will cease; as for knowledge, it will pass away. For we know in part and we prophesy in part, but when the perfect comes, the partial will pass away. When I was a child, I spoke like a child, I thought like a child, I reasoned as a child. When I became a man, I gave up childish ways. For now we see in a mirror dimly, but then face to face. Now I know in part; then I shall know fully, even as I have been fully known. So now faith, hope and love abide, these three, but the greatest of these is love.

Graduation 2005 PG Dip Ed.

Gwen and husband Bill at a 90th Birthday Party 2011

Home on the farm 1998

In India on a Victoria University
Religious Studies tour circa 1985

In Beijing in 1989 on a Victoria University Religious Studies tour

At Teacher's Training College in 1943 age19

ABOUT THE AUTHOR

T he author grew up in a rural community where the spires of two churches dominated the small village. Though a good proportion of the community were not regular church goers, it was generally accepted that hers was a Christian country. Over her long lifetime, attitudes and beliefs have changed. Of recent years scholars have written that the God in which she and her forebears had believed is dead or only a delusion – that mankind needed to invent such an authority that could provide us with guidelines and rules for living, If we broke the rules the divine power would punish. The author's own experience has convinced her that our concept of God is not merely an invention, and she has felt the need to tell her own story giving evidence of a spiritual force that she believes has communicated with humans and the living world since their beginning whenever or however that was.

This story begins with the Charismatic movement within the Christian Church in the 1970s. The author saw herself only as an observer at a "Life in the Spirit" programme at a mainstream church in New Zealand during that decade. People of several other Christian denominations were also involved. Her subsequent experience of the "Blessing of the Holy Spirit," and various unasked – for "gifts" resulted in her admission to a psychiatric hospital, although personally, at that time, she was quite sure she was obeying God in all that she said and did.

Forty years on, and with falling numbers within parts of the Christian Church, this seems the right time for that experience to be handed on beyond her own church and denomination - and finally - to all the wandering flock who may be prepared to believe in a spiritual force for good in the world, but not in all the traditional teachings of the Christian Church or of other religions in the areas where those religions have evolved.

* * * * * * * *

Educational qualifications

The author's experience at that time convinced her of the existence of this spiritual force - an existence of which she had become unsure over her adult years and so had never been prepared to teach others, but now she was persuaded to teach Sunday School in her local church, and "Bible in School" as a volunteer teacher in state schools.

After having gained a Certificate of Religious Knowledge from the Church Education Commission, and twenty years of teaching "Bible in School" and Sunday School, the author went back to University in 1995 to finish a B.A. that she had started in 1941, but had abandoned because of the war, majoring now in world religions with philosophy and ethics. She then gained a Graduate Diploma in Subject Studies for Teachers (Christian Education) doing papers including "Religion and Current Issues," "Issues in Christian History," "Issues in Christian Thought," "Curriculum development in Christian Education," and finally in 2005, a Post Graduate Diploma of Education, specialising in Social Studies. Papers taken for this qualification were – "Current issues in the teaching of Social Studies," "Ethics in Education," "Environmental Education," and "Curriculum Design."

Her main work over recent years has been producing resource material in the field of "values" education, for schools in a newly multi-cultural society. These lessons are based not on the teachings of any particular religion, but on reason, experience and ethical principles. They can be found on her website – www.valueseducation.co.nz

Examples – *Simple Ethical Skills: for use in a Multicultural Society. Forty Lessons on Citizenship.*

Printed in the United States
By Bookmasters